The Most Wonderful Writing Lessons Ever

Everything You Need to Teach the Essential
Elements—and the Magic—of Good Writing

· ·

by Barbara Mariconda

SCHOLASTIC
PROFESSIONAL BOOKS

New York • Toronto • London • Auckland • Sydney

DEDICATION

To a companion on the journey, Linda Hartzer—
for her vision, her wisdom, and her support

ACKNOWLEDGEMENTS

This book and the ideas and lessons within its covers would not have been possible without the dedication and commitment of the professional educators I have had the privilege of working with. The input and feedback of our Mill Hill School faculty in Southport, Connecticut, certainly helped shape this writing program—and their delivery of this program to children was what made it really work.

I would like to thank these talented, loving professionals for their insights, support, and contributions that helped this program evolve. Thanks to:

❖ *Our principal Linda Hartzer, whose love and concern for children fueled her vision for this program, not only in theory but in the kinds of concrete support that allowed the program to be a success.*

❖ *Donna Coble, our language arts specialist, for her tireless support and professional expertise.*

❖ *My grade-level colleagues, Pam Braus, Dea Paoletta Auray, and Kim Hastings, for the many gifts and talents they brought to the task and generously shared.*

❖ *Pat Ondek, who also served on our writing committee, for her forthright opinions and candid observations.*

❖ *Our grade three staff: Nancy Carlin, Carolyn Bourque, Christine Skogg, Marie Csom, Laurie Christensen, and Joan Hellthaler for their excellent feedback and willingness to put theory into action.*

❖ *Linda Chandler, for her technical support and constant interest and encouragement.*

❖ *Mary Santilli for believing in me.*

❖ *Marie Jordan Whitney, language arts coordinator for the Town of Fairfield.*

❖ *And again, to Dea Paoletta Auray for her vision, sense of humor, and hard work in launching our consulting firm, Empowering Magical Writes, enabling us to share our approach with a larger audience.*

❖ *The children of Mill Hill School, who taught me so, so much, and also....*

❖ *My husband Nick and my family for their undying encouragement and support.*

In an effort to bring this information to a wider audience, my partner, Dea Paoletta Auray, and I have formed a consulting firm called Empowering Magical Writes. We present the ideas in this book at workshops and seminars for educators.

For information on workshops and seminars on the Magical Writes approach, call or FAX (203) 374-8125 or write:
Empowering Magical Writes, P.O. Box 4, Easton, CT 06612

Front cover design by Kathy Massaro
Interior design by Sydney Wright
Interior photographs by Glen Mariconda Photography

ISBN 0-590-87304-0
Copyright © 1999 by Barbara Mariconda, all rights reserved.
Printed in USA

CONTENTS

Introduction

For me, writing has always been magical—the way the spell of a story, the enchantment of books, the power of words could transport me to another time, another place, letting me enter into another life.

I began writing in the third grade and have pursued writing with a passion ever since. Writing has been my vehicle for self-discovery, a means of defining how I look at the world and my relationships in it.

By the time I'd published about a dozen books for children, I took on a new role—as a second grade classroom teacher and as a *teacher* of writing.

Now writing itself presents a number of challenges—the self-discipline, the isolation, the rejection letters, the long periods of waiting that are typical of the publishing business. However, I discovered that teaching a class of seven- and eight-year-olds to write was often even more difficult.

Besides actually having my students get thoughts and words down on the page, I found myself faced with challenging classroom issues around methodology, management, and motivation. I'd have some children who generated numerous story topics but had difficulty actually beginning a story. I had others who could quickly choose a topic but struggled with translating a basic story idea into a fully elaborated piece of writing. Others wrote epic stories that lacked focus and seemed to ramble on endlessly.

It was also a challenge for me to keep track of individual student progress. I used checklists to keep track of where children were in their respective pieces, what mini-lessons I'd taught them, and what their individual assessed needs were. These checklists always seemed cumbersome and difficult to keep organized and current. And, despite my best efforts at encouraging independent work and peer conferencing, I often experienced what I call the "hotdog stand effect"—a group of students at my desk waiting on line, all of them saying, "I need a conference!" It was impossible to get to everyone in an efficient, timely way. We all wound up feeling frustrated—and our writing time often felt a little less than magical.

While I was struggling to manage my classroom writing program, many states (including Connecticut, Vermont, Massachusetts, and Florida) began administering State Mastery Tests to students in grades 4, 6, and 8. One section of this test was designed to assess basic writing skills. Connecticut students are required to write to a given prompt in a 45-minute block of time. Their responses are scored holistically. Fourth graders write a narrative, sixth graders an expository piece, and eighth graders a persuasive piece.

This was the first attempt by states to assess writing in some kind of consistent, objective way. The intent was to use test data to identify student needs and improve instruction. Despite the many innovations in the instruction of writing, the results of these tests have been very disappointing, with the majority of students scoring well below state goals. This suggested to me that perhaps I was not the only teacher struggling with writing instruction in my classroom.

In 1993, at Mill Hill School in Fairfield, Connecticut (where I taught second grade), only 47% of our fourth grade students met the state goal in narrative writing. In view of our scores, Mill Hill School formed a writing committee under the leadership of our principal, Linda Hartzer. Our goal was to identify weaknesses and devise a comprehensive program in response to these needs. My task would be to focus on the instruction of narrative writing in grades 2 and 3.

I decided that I would approach this as objectively as I could, applying everything I'd learned about writing and revision. I referred to the body of literature on the craft of writing—books by people like John Gardner, Joseph Campbell, and Jack Bickham— to help me define our writing needs and the ways in which we might address them. I analyzed hundreds of student pieces and looked closely at the instruction of narrative writing in grades 2 and 3. This led me to the following conclusions:

❖ Each teacher interpreted "writing as a process" differently and thus delivered the program in vastly different ways.

❖ There was little consistency across or between grade levels in writing instruction.

❖ There was little consistency in vocabulary and terminology across and between grade levels, resulting in student (and teacher) confusion.

❖ While teachers could certainly distinguish good writing from less-than-satisfactory writing, they had few *specific* strategies on how to move children forward.

❖ Most student writing lacked focus, elaborative detail, voice, and a clear "sense of story."

My objective was to design lessons that would instruct both *teachers and students in specific skills* that all good writers possess. Without clear definitions of what these skills are, teachers and students cannot be expected to recognize, demonstrate, apply, or assess writing skills in consistent, meaningful ways. My program would provide clear expectations, opportunities for continual assessment, and consistency across and between grade levels. The focus would be on whole-class instruction followed by the application of skills to process pieces.

In his classic book *The Art of Fiction: Notes on Craft for Young Writers*, John Gardner says: "Fiction is made of structural units; it is not one great rush. Every story is built of a number of such units: a passage of description, a passage of dialogue, an action, another passage of description, more dialogue, and so forth. The good writer treats each unit individually, developing them one by one." Gardner helped me see that each skill (writing an entertaining beginning, generating elaborative detail, building suspense, elaborating on a single significant main event, writing an effective, extended story ending) might be better taught and practiced *in isolation*. Artists and musicians do the same thing as they develop and grow—an artist learns and practices composition, form, and perspective before setting the brush to the canvas; a pianist learns scales and arpeggios before tackling a sonata. I believed that, similarly, skill lessons can be built upon one another in a *logical sequence* with clear-cut lessons for teachers to follow. In this way students could set about writing with these skills up their sleeves, thus eliminating a good amount of the frustrating revision work that results from a conference and mini-lesson *after* the first draft.

Therefore, the format for whole class instruction became:

❖ <u>**The Introduction of a new skill**</u> The teacher defines the skill and highlights it by pointing it out in pieces of high-quality literature.

❖ <u>**Modeling**</u> The teacher models each specific skill in isolation (Teacher as Author).

❖ <u>**Guided Practice**</u> Students practice the specific skill or technique in isolation.

❖ <u>**Application**</u> Students apply the skill to their own writing.

After designing, implementing, and revising this program at Mill Hill School over four years, we found astounding results.

Grade 4	1993	1994	1995	1996	1997
Mill Hill*	47%	65%	75%	81%	92%

(*% of students meeting the state goal)

What held more magic for me than these scores was the fact that we became a real community of writers. We shared a common language with which to discuss writing. We began to truly see reading and writing as the flip sides of the same coin, and we began to read differently—with what I call an "author's eye." Students were empowered by skills that enabled them to internalize the basic building blocks of writing, thus freeing themselves for what writing is *really* all about—using story as a means of tapping into the subconscious in deep and meaningful ways.

My purpose in writing this book is to share this successful, proven approach with you. My hope is that you will find the information, conversations, and classroom lessons and activities just what you need to help make your writing program come to life!

The spell of a story...the power of words...the magic of writing. This book does not contain incantations or sleights of hand. It contains the skills and building blocks, the patterns and frameworks that allow the magic to come forth. It contains the conversations, the bits of literature, the lessons, projects, and activities that bring the magic of writing alive. Now, let the magic begin!

What You Will Find in This Book

❖ An introduction to and definition of the following skill areas necessary for narrative writing:

> Writing entertaining beginnings
> Generating specific elaborate detail
> Building suspense
> Writing a fully elaborated main event
> Writing satisfying, extended story endings
> Using dialogue effectively

❖ Examples of each skill area from literature

❖ Scripted classroom lessons in each skill area

❖ Reproducible activity sheets

❖ Samples of student writing

❖ Long- and short-term writing projects for the application of each skill

❖ Suggestions on managing your writing program

CHAPTER 1

Using Literature for Prewriting

· · · · · · · · · · · · · · · · · ·

Reading With an Author's Eyes

A n ancient cave dweller paints a herd of bison on the wall of an underground cavern, documenting and celebrating a successful hunt. Pharaoh's scribes carve row after row of hieroglyphics on the lid of a sarcophagus, recording prayers and lists of the treasures that will follow him to the afterlife. A kindergartner presses down on a crayon, tongue peeking from the corner of her mouth, drawing a likeness of her house, each member of her family, and a scribble of random letters beneath it representing her feelings about them. Each of the authors—the cave dweller, the scribe, and the kindergartner—had a similar purpose: to leave a mark of some kind that would communicate thoughts, words, and images in the hope that someone else would see them and understand. There is a kind of magic that occurs when one's thoughts and feelings are translated into symbols that can be read and understood by others. Writing and reading, therefore, are inextricably connected—both necessary in order for the magic spell to be completed.

Writing has become more sophisticated since the time of the cave dwellers and pharaohs, and authors write for a variety of specific purposes. Writing was intended to record, inform, persuade, or entertain, but as the author's *purpose* changed, so did the nature of writing.

And not only does the nature of writing change depending on the author's purpose but so does the nature of reading. If the reader recognizes the author's purpose at the onset, he has a better chance of receiving the author's message. Therefore, a clear understanding of the purpose of a piece of writing is critical for both the author and the reader—for the author in organizing and constructing the piece and for the reader in comprehending it.

Purpose and Audience

In the first few years of school, children begin to move through the sequence of prewriting experiences such as drawing pictures, labeling, scribble writing, and on to writing short pieces using some sound-symbol relationships and, later, temporary and conventional spelling. The next step for many children is to experiment with journal writing. They use journals to write about where they've been, what they did, and how they felt about a variety of topics and experiences. Then children are often expected to use their journals as a source of topics for narrative writing.

This jump from journal entry to narrative story is sometimes difficult for students, as they might not have a clear understanding of *purpose*. When a child makes a journal entry, her purpose is usually to *record* and *reflect* on an experience or a feeling. And writing journal entries is not only different from the narrative in terms of purpose. The intended *audience* is also different: The narrative is written to entertain an audience of *others*, while, traditionally, the journal or diary entry is written to record and reflect on experiences for *oneself*. Unless journal writing has been established as an avenue for sharing with others, the translation of journal entry into narrative story can be troublesome.

Using Picture Books to Teach Genre

I begin the second-grade year with an extensive, intensive series of lessons that address the purpose and audience for the following genres of writing: journal writing/memoirs, two varieties of narrative, and expository writing. (Note: I do not address persuasive writing at this time.) What follows is an example of how I handle that all-important initial lesson on **genre, purpose,** and **audience.**

Before the lesson, I spend quite a bit of time selecting an assortment of narrative picture books and illustrated nonfiction/expository books. I also pull out my own journal. I make quite a show of setting these books up (in random order) on a display table in front of the room. The children buzz around the table like bees, picking up and examining books that interest them. I hang on to my journal, however, and refrain from adding it to the collection. This intrigues many of them.

"What do you have there, Mrs. Mariconda?" asks Sarah.

"I think it's her journal!" whispers Emily excitedly.

I raise an eyebrow and smile.

"You're right," I say. "This *is* my journal!"

They huddle around me.

"Can we see?" they beg.

I sit down and gather them around me.

"You know, boys and girls, journals are sometimes private," I say.

"Yeah," agrees Dan, "like a diary."

I nod. "Right. So, why do people write in journals? What kinds of things do they write?"

Their hands go up immediately. They share bits and pieces of the kinds of things they've recorded in their journals—a trip to Grandma's in Florida, a camp-out with a friend, deep feelings about the death of a beloved pet. I stop them there.

"So," I say, "it seems as though you use your journals to write down things you want to remember, things you want to reflect back on."

They nod.

I go on. "I'll bet that many of you have written about things in your journal that are private, things that are important to you alone." I pause. "There are some parts of my journal that I'd be happy to share with you," I say, "and other parts I prefer to keep private." I sit back. "*Who* do you think I wrote this journal for?"

They think about that for a moment.

"For yourself," says Amelia.

I nod. "That's right. I wrote it so that I can go back and read about things that are important to me."

I take a piece of chart paper and write:

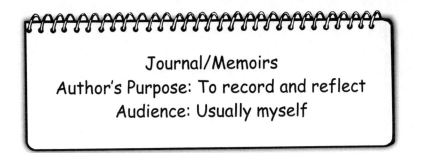

Journal/Memoirs
Author's Purpose: To record and reflect
Audience: Usually myself

I turn back toward the table full of books and hold up several examples of narrative stories.

"What about these?" I ask. "Why do you think the author wrote these books? What was the *author's purpose?*"

There is a buzz within the group as they try to put their ideas into words. Finally Michael says, "The author wrote them so we could read them and enjoy them."

"Yes," I say. I hold up a book with a comical cover. "This one was written to make you laugh." I hold up one with a spooky cover. "This one was written to make you scared. The author wrote these books to *entertain* you! We call these kinds of entertaining stories *narratives*." I get another piece of chart paper and write:

Narrative Stories
Author's Purpose: To Entertain
Audience: Others

Next I hold up several nonfiction expository books. Books with photographs or realistic drawings on the covers. Books with titles like *Amazing Spiders* and *Trains*.

"How are these books different?" I ask.

Peter tips his head this way and that, considering. "Those books are written to teach you stuff about spiders, or trains, or whatever they're about."

"That's right!" I say. "The author still wants you to enjoy the book, but the *purpose,* the reason, the author wrote the story, is to give you information! We call these nonfiction or *expository* books."

I get a third piece of chart paper and write:

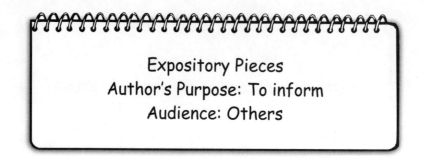

Expository Pieces
Author's Purpose: To inform
Audience: Others

"Now comes the fun part," I tell them. I mix-up all the narrative and expository books and make one big pile of them. Then I hold them up, one at a time. They read the title, look at the cover, and decide whether the book is narrative or expository. I stand them up on the chalk ledge in categories. Here are some of the titles and how the children divided them:

EXPOSITORY	NARRATIVE
All About Trees	*Brave Irene*
Pirates	*Owl Moon*
Lighthouses	*The Lighthouse Keeper's Daughter*
The Seashore	*Barn Dance*
Turkeys That Fly and Turkeys That Don't	*Tough Boris*
Amazing Spiders	*The Trouble With Mom*
Bees and Wasps	*All the Places to Love*
Tut's Mummy	*Little Red Riding Hood*

Simply by reading the title and looking at the cover design, the children could clearly recognize the author's purpose. What is interesting about this is that even though many of the narratives shared a common theme or topic with the expository pieces (such as *Lighthouses* and *The Lighthouse Keeper's Daughter*, and *Pirates* and *Tough Boris*), the children had no trouble deciding which was intended to give information and which was intended to entertain.

I hold my journal up. "Which pile should this go in?" I ask.

Some point hesitantly to the narrative pile, others to the expository pile, others refrain, withholding judgment.

Matt raises his hand, and I nod.

"I think it belongs in a separate pile," he says.

"Oh?" I ask, encouraging him to tell me more.

"These books are all written for other people," he says, gesturing toward the collection on the chalk ledge. "Your journal is written just for you."

"Ah..." I say. "Audience."

"Ooh! Ooh!" squeals Hanna. "I know something else."

"What's that?" I ask.

She points to the expository pile. "These are written to give information, and these," she says, pointing to the narratives, "are written to entertain us." She pauses. "But your journal is written so you'll remember stuff you want to think about later."

I nod. They've got it! Purpose and audience!

Two Kinds of Narratives

Once my students begin to understand the differences between journal entries, expository pieces, and narratives, I am ready to turn our attention to the narrative, as this is the genre they will be learning how to write. But before I could teach them, I had some questions for myself:

❖ What are the characteristics of a narrative story?
❖ How are narratives different from expository pieces?
❖ Are all narratives alike?

For answers I looked at children's literature, narrative picture books that I'd read aloud to my second graders, studying the underlying patterns on which the writing was constructed. To do this, students must learn how to read with "author's eyes."

> Readers and teachers are like visitors who've paid money to tour a famous home. Ah, readers say, what lovely rooms. Yes, the teacher says, notice the artful placement of the windows. Writers look at a story the way a carpenter or architect looks at a house: They see the surface but also the structure under the paint. They know how the house is put together and how much work it was to build.
> —Jesse Lee Kercheval, *Building Fiction*

By reading in the way Jesse Lee Kercheval describes—reading with author's eyes—I discovered that there are generally two kinds of narratives. The first is the most common and is constructed using the underlying framework of most traditional folk and fairy tales. This is what I call a **character/problem/solution narrative**. The emphasis is on the main character, some problem or struggle the main character undergoes, and finally, a solution brought about *by the main character*. This is an important point. The main character serves as a kind of hero in this type of story. The main character earns the reader's respect by struggling and overcoming problems. Even if the main character makes mistakes initially, this kind of story is characterized by growth and change—the main character grows and changes as a result of the struggle and the solution.

The second type of narrative story is what I call a **personal experience narrative**. The emphasis in this type of narrative is on the *experience*, rather than on the character. There is no need for a problem-solution sequence in the personal experience narrative because the emphasis is on the interesting, entertaining experience rather than on the character. These stories are often heavily descriptive.

The purpose of both these types of narrative is to entertain the audience.

I made an interesting discovery in analyzing these two types of narrative—a discovery I knew I could turn into an effective lesson for kids. Let's look at the list of narrative stories the children sorted through in the lesson on genre:

> <u>Brave Irene</u>
> Owl Moon
> <u>The Lighthouse Keeper's Daughter</u>
> Barn Dance
> <u>Tough Boris</u>
> <u>The Trouble With Mom</u>
> All the Places to Love
> <u>Little Red Riding Hood</u>

Notice the titles that are underlined. Is it a coincidence that each of the underlined titles is a narrative characterized by the character/problem/solution pattern? The focus of this kind of narrative is on *character.* Each underlined title clearly hints at that focus—the titles themselves consist of the main character's names. Not only do these titles point to the main character, but many of them hint at the problem component; for instance, Babette Cole's hysterical tale: *The **Trouble** With Mom*—sounds like a problem, doesn't it? And William Steig's classic, ***Brave Irene***—if she's brave, she must have encountered a problem! How about Mem Fox's ***Tough Boris***—problems tend to toughen people up a bit, don't they?

And what about the titles that were not underlined? As the title of Jane Yolen's *Owl Moon* suggests, this is a personal experience narrative that focuses on an occurrence rather than on a character with a problem. The story is about going owling in the moonlight. Yolen never reveals the character's name or gender. The focus is on the *experience* of walking in the winter woods looking for owls. Bill Martin's *Barn Dance* is another personal experience story. It is about a boy (nameless!) who ventures into the barn one night and takes part in a magical dance with all of the farm animals. Again, the focus is on the *experience* and not the character. Patricia MacLachlan's picture book *All the Places to Love* describes a beloved farm and all the places there to love and remember, focusing on setting and experience, *not* character.

These are important distinctions because children can learn, on the basis of title alone, to make fairly accurate predictions about stories before they begin reading or listening. We read them aloud, discuss them, analyze them, and summarize them. They learn to read with author's eyes, watching for the underlying pattern of character/problem/solution or personal experience. The awareness of the pattern makes it easier for them to later assimilate these characteristics into their own writing.

Once they are familiar with the two types of narrative, children become quite vocal about their observations. Often, as I read aloud, I hear comments like: "Uh oh, that sounds like a *problem!*" While reading on, I hear some of them remark, "Oh no, the problem's getting even *worse!*" As the main character struggles, the rapt expressions on their faces tell me that they're busy making predictions, striving to solve the problem ahead of the main character, and are visibly relieved when the character ultimately triumphs. (I particularly like to use Steig's *Brave Irene* for this purpose.)

With this heightened awareness of the underlying patterns of each type of narrative, *every reading and listening experience becomes a writing lesson as well!* What a wonderful rehearsal for constructing their own narrative stories.

Classifying and Summarizing Pieces of Writing

Many books contain a summary at the beginning—usually a one sentence blurb that appears below the Library of Congress Cataloging in Publication Data on the copyright page. This can be a terrific resource for the writing teacher.

Here's how I use story summaries.

SUMMARIES – THE LEAST COMMON DENOMINATORS

1. Show the cover of the book to the class.
2. Have students predict the genre (character/problem/solution, personal experience, or expository) on the basis of title and cover design.
3. Read the book aloud to them and compare predictions to actual story.
4. Read the story summary (what I call reducing the story to its least common denominator) on the copyright page. Discuss how a summary differs from a fully elaborated story.

Here are a few examples as they appear on the copyright page of each book. The first three are all examples of character/problem/solution stories:

Officer Buckle and Gloria by Peggy Rathmann
<u>Summary</u>: The children at Napville Elementary School always ignore Officer Buckle's safety tips, until a police dog named Gloria accompanies him when he gives his safety speeches.

Uglypuss by Caroline Gregoire
<u>Summary</u>: Marty has always longed for a pet dog, but when he finally gets one, he's so ugly that Marty doesn't even want him around.

Eggbert, the Slightly Cracked Egg by Tom Ross
<u>Summary</u>: A cracked egg with a talent for painting goes through some painful experiences before realizing that being cracked can be something to be proud of.

Notice how each of these summaries focuses on the *character* and the *problem*. The next summaries are for personal experience stories:

Country Road by Daniel San Souci
<u>Summary</u>: A walk with Dad along the old country road one day in spring brings sightings of a hawk, fox tracks, a school of trout, and other signs of nature.

All I See by Cynthia Rylant
<u>Summary</u>: A child paints with an artist friend, who sees and paints only whales.

Encounter by Jane Yolen
<u>Summary</u>: A Taino Indian boy on the island of San Salvador recounts the landing of Columbus and his men in 1492.

Notice how the summaries of these stories focus on an *experience* and the related observations, rather than a character. Notice too that the characters mentioned in each summary remain nameless. Character is secondary to the experience in this type of story.

Finally, look at these summaries of expository books:

Into the Mummy's Tomb by Nicholas Reeves
<u>Summary</u>: An account of Howard Carter's discovery of the tomb of King Tutankhamen, descriptions of the artifacts inside and their importance, the discovery in 1988 of more artifacts, and theories about the curse associated with the tomb.

Frogs by Gail Gibbons
<u>Summary</u>: An introduction to frogs, discussing their tadpole beginnings, noises they make, their hibernation, body parts, and how they differ from toads.

Amazing Spiders by Alexandra Parsons

Summary: Text and photographs introduce some of the most amazing members of the spider family, such as fish-eating spiders, spitting spiders, and banana spiders.

Each of these expository summaries focuses on information. Clue words like *introduce*, *discuss*, and *an account of* are indications of author's purpose.

Summarizing stories and classifying them by genre are related skills, critical for both readers and writers. By classifying a story as expository, character/problem/solution narrative, or personal experience narrative, we also identify and define the intended purpose, audience, organization, and focus of the piece.

Having students summarize what they've heard or read is a valuable prewriting and planning tool: If students can sum up the story they hope to write in a sentence or two, chances are better that their story direction and focus will be clear.

With this in mind, I provided my students with three different generic formats for summarizing that would help them identify the characteristics of each genre. These formats could also be used to help students plan what they'd like to write.

I display these formats on posters in the classroom for daily reference throughout the school year. We use them to classify and summarize every time we read together. I also photocopy these formats for students to use as prewriting tools.

Character/Problem/Solution Narrative	Character/Problem/Solution Narrative
Name:	Name:
This is a story about _____ (main character's name)	This is a story about _a teacher named Miss Nelson._ (main character's name)
The problem was that _____ (describe problem)	The problem was that _her class always misbehaved._ (describe problem)
The problem was solved when _____ (tell how main character solves the problem)	The problem was solved when _Miss Nelson comes disguised as the mean Elvira Swamp and teaches them a lesson._ (tell how main character solves the problem)

I model the use of this format for summarizing as often as possible, dropping in the critical components of each story we read. For example, can you guess what story I'm summarizing here? Of course you've recognized the story. It's Harry Allard's classic, *Miss Nelson Is Missing.* The title and summary address character, problem, and solution.

Here is the format I use for summarizing a personal experience narrative

Personal Experience Narrative

Name: _____

This is a story that describes _____
an experience or a place
_____
_____

First, _____
Describe what happens in the BEGINNING of the story
_____
_____
_____

Next, _____
Describe what happens in the MIDDLE of the story

Personal Experience Narrative

Name: _____

This is a story that describes *a father and child's*
an experience or a place
nighttime outing in the woods to see a
great horned owl.

First, *they set out in the forest*
Describe what happens in the BEGINNING of the story
_____
_____
_____

Next, *they call the owl*
Describe what happens in the MIDDLE of the story

> Can you name the story based on my summary? Any children's librarian or bookseller—and many an avid reader—could tell you in a second that the book I'm summarizing is Jane Yolen's *Owl Moon*.

And, finally, the expository summarizing format:

Expository Piece

Name: _____

This piece gives information about _____
the topic
_____

Including _____
a main idea
_____
_____
_____
_____

_____
another main idea
_____
_____
_____
_____

and _____
another main idea
_____

Expository Piece

Name: _____

This piece gives information about *bats*
the topic
_____

Including *what they look like*
a main idea
_____
_____
_____
_____

how they behave
another main idea
_____
_____
_____

and *where they live*
another main idea
_____

> The use of this summarizing format leaves little room for doubt about the book described. You could probably guess the title of this book, even if you've never read it. It is called *Bats: Creatures of the Night* by Joyce Milton.

Write-Read-Write: The Magical Cycle

Any teacher will attest that it is very difficult to separate reading and writing. These two acts are truly flip sides of the same coin. We write so that our audience will read, and when we read (if we're attentive enough), we can learn quite a bit about how stories are crafted. And thus, the magical cycle continues.

However, this reading-writing connection alone, powerful though it is, is not enough of a basis on which to build strong writing skills. Constructing a summary is a far cry from constructing an entertaining narrative. Becoming a skillful writer does not happen by magic or by osmosis. This "magical cycle" must be analyzed and nurtured.

The skills described in this chapter—identifying the author's purpose and audience, classifying a piece of writing by its distinguishing characteristics, and summarizing a piece of writing in a way that reflects the unique characteristics of its genre—are but the *first steps* on the magical journey.

Teaching Children the Pattern of a Story

· · · · · · · · · · · · · · · · · ·

or, Where Is This Story Going? Give Me a Road Map, Please!

A child in your class works diligently on a magical adventure story of almost epic proportions. The main character in this epic blasts off into space, fights alien armies, ventures into a black hole, flies through a time machine, winds up back in the days of the dinosaurs, battles T-Rex, meets a caveman army...but despite all this, the story never really seems to *go* anywhere. It's long on action, short on detail. It rambles on with no promise of any kind of relevant, meaningful ending. The child continues adding new adventures in an attempt to reach some level of satisfaction with the story, but a general sense of frustration sets in.

Certainly the problem is not a lack of effort or of interest, that's for sure. But this story is languishing, and you're not sure how to help the young author get it back on track. What is it, exactly, that makes for that satisfying sense of story—that seemingly elusive quality that draws the reader in, pulls us along, encourages us to predict and anticipate the plot, and finally carries us along to a fulfilling conclusion?

The answer is *pattern*.

Should we provide children with a pattern for their narrative writing before they set their pencils to the page? I believe the answer is a resounding YES!

Here is the best analogy I can think of to support this idea. Imagine that I am standing before a group of my peers (you included), and I'm complimented on my lovely, stylish blazer. You comment on the smart cut, the shape of the lapels, the double-breasted design. I say, "Great, I'm thrilled that you like it!" With an enthusiastic smile, I inform you that now you will have an opportunity to make a lovely, stylish blazer like mine! We list the attributes and characteristics of my blazer that you'd mentioned earlier, I hand out fabric, thread, and pins, and I send you off to the nearest sewing machine.

"But..." you begin, "I don't really know what to do...."

"Don't worry about that," I tell you, "just think about what you like about this blazer and start there. Later we'll have a conference to discuss your work."

Most likely, the majority of the group would be lost and fumbling. I'd meet to confer with each of you, ask you questions, and take out that seam ripper to facilitate the necessary modifications. (It might take me quite a long time to meet with all of you, so I hope you'll be patient. Perhaps you could confer with one of your peers within the group in the meantime.)

It would be my guess that after our initial conference and after pulling a thousand stitches or so, you, along with most of the group, would be ready to chuck the botched blazer and head for the mall!

Wouldn't it have been easier to distribute a pattern in the first place and proceed from there? It's true, the pattern would definitely produce a more predictable product. But at least we would recognize it as what it was supposed to be—a jacket! Once completed, couldn't the designer make creative modifications? And furthermore, after creating several other jackets using that basic pattern, I'll bet that many participants would internalize that pattern, learn the procedure, and go on to create their own innovative design, packed with personal style and flair. *Yet, it would still resemble a jacket in all of the essential ways!*

In essence, we put children in a similar position when we set them to a narrative writing task without first presenting them with the basic narrative pattern and the skills necessary to use it.

Here's What the Experts Say About Pattern

As I began my own personal journey and training as a writer, I read everything I could on the elements of effective fiction writing. Time and time again the subject of pattern came up. This information proved invaluable to me and laid the groundwork for each manuscript that I sold. I believe that this knowledge is critical for *all* teachers and students of writing. Here is what just a few of the experts have to say about the role of pattern in fiction.

Author, educator, **Ronald Tobias**, in his book *Theme and Strategy*: "Patterns are fundamental to human nature. We like to create them (the arts) and we like to discover them (the sciences). In writing these two powerful forces combine: as artists we create the patterns, but we create them for our audiences to find…Creativity is fluid and, like water, it is formless and always conforms to the container that holds it. If there's no vessel to contain the water, then it will run off and drain endlessly. Such is the danger of having too little or no preconception of the story you want to write."

The late **Joseph Campbell**, world-renowned expert on mythology, referring to the main character and plot in *The Power of Myth*: "You leave the world that you're in and go into a depth or into a distance or up to a height. There you come to what was missing in your consciousness in the world you formerly inhabited. That's the basic motif of the universal hero's journey—leaving one condition and finding the source of life to bring you forth into a richer or mature condition."

I heard Newbery Award-winning author **Lois Lowry** echo Campbell's ideas at the Society of Children's Book Writers and Illustrators' twenty-fifth national conference in Los Angeles. She used an analogy of patterns and music, stating that a story, like a piece of classical music, begins at a place of rest (exposition), moves through a series of complications (the development section), and returns to a place of rest (recapitulation), but with at least one essential variation or change.

Also in *Theme and Strategy*, twentieth century philosopher **Alfred North Whitehead** talks about art as pattern imposed upon experience. Real life is chaotic, unpredictable, and random. Fiction, on the other hand, is sequential, deliberate, built on a highly selective series of cause-and-effect events.

The use of a framework or pattern assists the author in selecting events and shaping them in relevant ways.

Patterns for Student Writing

It seemed to me, then, that I needed to provide my students with a workable pattern that would help them draw upon their personal experience and extend these ideas into entertaining narrative stories. Initially, the pattern I provided them with looked something like this:

- ❖ Put the character in a setting.
- ❖ Give the character a problem.
- ❖ Make the problem worse.
- ❖ Then solve the problem.

I encouraged my students to plan their narrative stories using this pattern as their prewriting framework. I provided them with a "blueprint" or map to fill in as part of their prewriting/ planning that looked like this:

PATTERNS FOR STUDENT WRITING

This story is about ———————————————————————————— .
 a character in a setting

The problem was that ———————————————————————————— .

It got even worse when ———————————————————————————— .

Finally, the problem was solved when ———————————————————

—— .

It looks good, doesn't it? But to my surprise, it didn't work.

What follows is an example of the typical kind of story this pattern generated. This one was written by a second grader using the framework above. The bold-faced comments are mine.

One cloudy day I went for a walk in the woods with my dog Buffy. *(A character in a setting.)* It was nice there. But Buffy chased a squirrel and then she was lost. *(That's a problem!)* I looked for her and called her but I couldn't find Buffy anywhere. I was so sad and upset. It was getting dark. *(The problem gets worse!)* So I went home very sad and crying. I told my mom and dad, and dad went out with the car looking for Buffy. Finally he found her and brought her home. *(The problem is solved.)* I was so happy to have Buffy home!

THE END

It fits the pattern all right—has a character, a problem, and a solution. It had a logical beginning, middle, and ending. But, well, it's...*boring*. It doesn't work as well as it might have for several reasons. If this story were based on an actual personal experience, it would certainly have relevance for the *author*. But remember, the purpose of narrative writing is to *entertain an audience of others*!

Also, kids are accustomed to having adults solve their problems for them. In *real life*, having the responsible adult solve the problem works; in the world of fiction, *the main character must struggle to solve the problem*. In this story, the main character (the child) did not solve the problem.

Still, it seemed to me that this story plan was one that *could* work. I began to think through the *what-ifs* that authors use in constructing their stories. The what-ifs, I was sure, could transform this story into something special.

What if...

❖ the author *showed* us how adorable Buffy was—showed us his fluffy brown fur, his huge sad eyes, his scruffy, waggily tail?

❖ we could *see* the main character's feelings of distress and sadness when Buffy got lost—the quivering bottom lip, the pounding heart, the tears welling up?

❖ we shared the main character's worries and fears—that perhaps someone stole Buffy, that he could get hit by a car or be lost forever?

❖ we accompanied the main character on his search for Buffy—heard the main character calling him until his throat was sore, walked beside the main character as he trudged the streets searching, until his feet were hot and blistered?

❖ Dad finally does come along to help? (Wouldn't we feel as though, after all of that struggling, the main character earned his help?)

❖ at the end, the main character learned something from the experience and made a decision based on what happened?

I knew that *I* could certainly use the what-ifs to beef up the Buffy story, but I wondered whether it was possible to empower my students with these skills. I decided to find out by designing a pattern that would address the what-ifs.

Keeping in mind the what-ifs, I assessed hundreds of second and third grade student papers to identify common needs.

Here's what I found:

❖ The majority of student work I looked at had weak, predictable beginnings. ("One sunny day...", "One dark night....", "Hi, my name is....", "This is a story about...").

❖ There was little elaborative detail to draw the reader in. Details tended to be general rather than specific. (Adjectives like *nice, cool,* and *pretty* abounded.) There were often extraneous details that didn't add to the story ("He wore blue pants, a striped shirt, and brown shoes"—what I call "police blotter" details).

❖ There seemed to be a lack of focus and little momentum, suspense, or anticipation leading to some *meaningful* main event. Often the stories consisted of lists of events that could be resequenced in any order whatsoever without affecting the outcome in any significant way.

❖ The main character did not grow or change in any notable way as a result of the main event.

❖ The endings were abrupt—*very* abrupt: "And so I went home and went to bed. THE END."

To help my student writers out these common writing ruts, I came up with a "gem" of a graphic organizer.

As you can see on the next page, the diamond's very shape illustrates the proportion of story elements in relation to one another. The main event commands the most attention by virtue of the area that it takes up relative to the whole story. This is where the writer spends the most time. The diamond shape also shows a build-up toward the middle of the story, with the main event being at the widest part. The diamond shape reflects Joseph Campbell's and Lois Lowry's observations about the "going and coming" that shape all effective stories, with the story beginning at a place of rest (establishment of setting) at the top point of the diamond, growing in tension and complication to the expansive middle section (the main event), and then returning to a place similar to where the story began (a conclusion and reflective ending) at the bottom. The diamond also calls for specific kinds of elaboration that bring the story to life and move the plot forward, and suggests cohesion (story focus) rather than a series of events running in linear fashion.

The Narrative Writing Diamond

This framework is meant to be used as a **guide**, not a set-in-stone rule. For example, a story might begin at home, in an ordinary, uninteresting setting. In that case, the author would not describe it. However, the basic story proportions remain constant, and in every story, the main event deserves the most attention! For the beginning author, this is a proven sequence that shapes their work successfully.

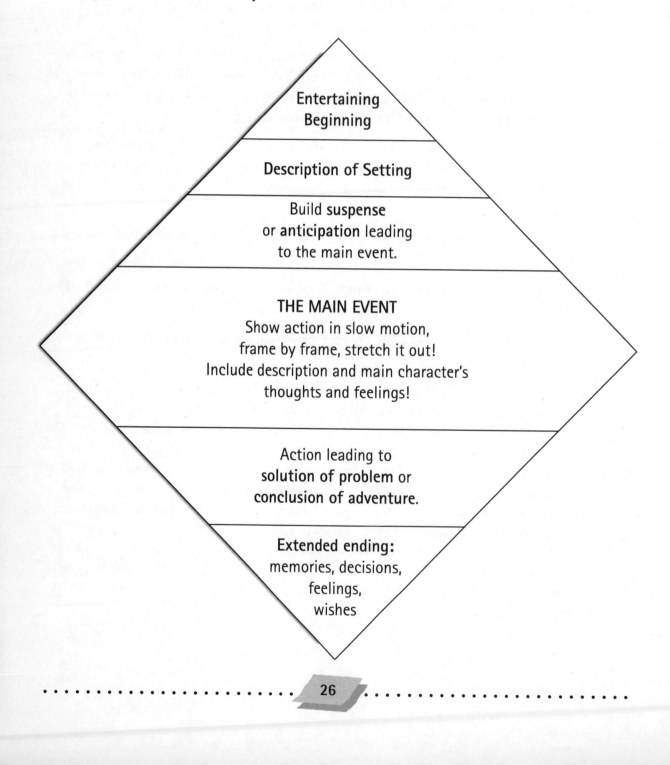

Entertaining
Beginning

Description of Setting

Build **suspense**
or **anticipation** leading
to the main event.

THE MAIN EVENT
Show action in slow motion,
frame by frame, stretch it out!
Include description and main character's
thoughts and feelings!

Action leading to
solution of problem or
conclusion of adventure.

Extended ending:
memories, decisions,
feelings,
wishes

Quality Writing: Like a Fine Gem

Diamonds are valued for their quality and brilliance. They are rated on the four characteristics of color, clarity, cut, and carat weight (the 4 c's!). Good writing is also valued for its quality! We can compare quality writing to a fine gem.

◆ **Color** is added to our writing through description and elaboration.

◆ **Clarity** comes through effective word choice, allowing the reader to understand what we have written.

◆ **Cut** is achieved by knowing what to leave out and what to include in a story.

◆ **Carat weight**—be sure to "weigh" and compare the various story elements for an effective whole.
   Color + Clarity + Cut + Carat weight = Brilliance!

—Nancy Carlin, a colleague of mine who used the writing diamond in her third grade class

The Writing Diamond: Getting Started

Remember the sewing analogy? Let's assume you have the pattern—a Vogue pattern all folded neatly into a handy packet. Smooth sailing now, right?

Smoother, maybe, than it would have been without the pattern at all, but you wouldn't be out of the woods yet. Now it's time for a series of sewing lessons—translations and definitions of the signs and symbols, and some practice with specific skills. You would learn the sewing skills in a logical sequence—in the sequence that they are typically used. First, the skill would be introduced and defined, then it would be modeled, then you'd practice the skill in isolation, and *then* apply it to your jacket!

In this very same way, I use the writing diamond to introduce writing skills in a logical sequence—in the sequence that they are typically used within the context of a story. I show students the writing diamond and point out the various sections and the relationships between them. I'll ask them questions such as:

❖ Why is it important for a story beginning, short as it is, to be entertaining? (*If it weren't, the reader would not read on.*)

❖ Why is the setting important? (*It establishes a place for the characters to act.*)

❖ What IS suspense, and why do you enjoy it?

❖ What section of the story do you think takes the author the longest to write and contains the most important details? (*The main event*)

❖ How is a conclusion different from an ending?

I explain that we will be learning about each section of the writing diamond, from top to bottom. I display the diamond in the room (usually drawn on a large poster board) and refer to it as we move along.

Developing the "Magic"

On the next page is an example of a second grader's story, written in a 45-minute time block in response to a prompt assigned as an assessment. This was after several months of instruction in which *each segment* of the writing diamond was presented and practiced in isolation and applied to process pieces.

Note the way in which the diamond pattern shaped this student's story. Imagine where this unrevised draft could go if the student had the opportunity to confer with the teacher, revisit the piece, and revise! This student demonstrates a good understanding of the narrative framework and has a solid foundation on which to let her creativity flow freely.

Crunch, crunch! The ruff leaves crackled under my feet. I saw tall, brown trunked trees that stood over me like giants. I hered the birds chirping soft, sweet sounds that sounded like music. I felt the cool wind blowing agenst my check. My nose snifed a butiful red rose. All of a sudden I heard a rustling sound in the bushes. I peered into the bushes. That was when I saw it! It had a dark blue dress with twinkeling purpel stars on it. She had rosie red checks and big blue ...

The opening of Emily's story.

Emily's Story

Crunch, crunch! The rough leaves cracked under my feet. I saw tall, brown-trunked trees that stood over me like giants. I heard the birds chirping soft, sweet sounds that sounded like music. I felt the cool wind blowing against my cheek. My nose sniffed a beautiful red rose. All of a sudden I heard a rustling sound in the bushes. I peered into the bushes. That was when I saw it! It had a dark blue dress with twinkling purple stars on it. She had rosy red cheeks and big blue eyes. She had a set of pale wings that shined in the sun. And in her hand was a golden wand. It was a...a...a... FAIRY! "Are you a fairy?" I asked. My mouth dropped open, my eyes got big and wide. I was shocked. "Yes," she said. "I will grant you one wish." "I wish I could go back in time to see...to see...the dinosaurs!" "Are you sure you want to wish for that?" asked the fairy. "Yes!" I said. "OK," she said. "Your wish is granted." Suddenly we were back in time, to the dinosaurs! "Bye," called the fairy. "Wait!" I yelled. But she didn't hear me. "I guess I'm on my own," I said. I looked around me. Stegosauruses chomped on plants and whacked at trees with their tails. Pterodactyls flew over my head and swooped down to the water for food. Triceratops charged at rocks and protected their young. Long-necked brontosauruses cooled themselves off in the stream. I climbed onto one and rode it. "Weeeee!" I yelled. Suddenly we heard a loud noise. BOOM, BOOM, GRRRR! All of a sudden, a tyrannosaurus rex ran out of a bush. Everyone ran, including me. But the T-rex saw me. He ran after me. "Ahhh!" I screamed. "Help me, somebody, ahh! Help me, fairy, help me!" All of a sudden the fairy appeared. "Help me, fairy, help me," I begged. The fairy waved her magic wand over me. Soon I was invisible. The T-rex turned around in the other direction to look for something else to eat. "Can I go back to my house?" I said. "But you can only have one wish," said the fairy. "Please, please, please," I said. "All right," she said. She waved her magic wand, and soon I was back at my house. I felt safe and relieved that I was back home. I still remember that fairy. I wish she was still here. I decided that I would never wish to go back to the dinosaur time again.

> One day I went to
> my grandmother's farm, She
> asked me to milk the cow
> so I went into the
> barn to milk the cow wen
> I herd a noise I went
> to the corner to see what

FIRST WEEK STORY

One day I went to my grandmother's farm. She asked me to milk the cow, so I went into the barn to milk the cow, when I heard a noise. I went to the corner to see what it was. It was a puppy. It was a very cute puppy. My grandmother let me keep him. I named him Rover. The End.

Here is another example that clearly shows skills developing over time. The story above was a timed attempt written by a boy during the first week of second grade. It's a simple personal experience narrative with a clear-cut beginning, middle, and end. There is no specific detail and no real evidence of any parts of the writing diamond. What follows on page 31 is another timed prompt about a magical sled by the same student, written in December. Note the improvements in the specific skill areas taught—writing an entertaining beginning, building suspense, and writing specific elaborative detail.

The best pieces of narrative writing seem to have an almost magical flow that carries the reader into the story, linking events in a meaningful way. The author—like a magician with a clever sleight-of-hand—draws the reader into the story, creating an illusion that makes the fictional world seem real.

> The Magicl Ride (part)
>
> I was outside on a wintery day. It was iccy cold and light white and the sky was white like snow. I was haveing fun in the cold snow when I saw a gold and silver thing withe bright perple, green and *+turqcose blue diments And It stood on a orenge platform. It seemed to have weeles on the botum of it. It started to move and I wondered why. I felt

But for both the author and the magician, the illusion depends on a sequence of skills, a pattern of action, practiced and assimilated to the point that they become invisible to the audience.

The magic is in knowing the pattern and putting it to use!

DECEMBER STORY

The Magic Ride

I was outside on a wintry day. It was icy cold and light white and the sky was white like snow. I was having fun in the cold snow, when I saw a gold and silver thing with bright purple, green, and turquoise blue diamonds. And it stood on an orange platform. It seemed to have wheels on the bottom of it. It started to move, and I wondered why. I felt like sitting and wanted to sit on it, so I did. Suddenly it moved, and I was riding down a hill like a rocket. Wow! Suddenly a steering wheel and a seat belt came up. I held on tight. Suddenly somehow I did a flip. Cool! Ouch! I fell off, in so much pain I could hardly get up. But I did. I got on again and held tighter and didn't fall off. That was a fun ride, but I was getting tired. I told it to take me home, and it did. I went inside. I'd never forget that day.

CHAPTER 3

Compelling Beginnings

. . . .

or, First Impressions Count!

It's true—first impressions mean a lot. Think back for a moment. Have you ever attended a party and been introduced to someone who greeted you with a noncommittal, limp, dead-fish kind of handshake? Or met a person who avoids eye contact and nervously scans the room during your introduction? Sometimes being on the receiving end of an introduction of this sort makes you wish you had a magic wand that could—*abracadabra*—make you just disappear!

There is a parallel here to reading and writing. When a reader picks up a book and thumbs to the first page, authors have the opportunity to introduce the reader to their fictional world and make a first impression. If that opening is noncommittal, unclear, confusing, or boring, there often is no second chance—the reader shuts the book, returns it to the shelf, and looks for a book that starts off with a bang, or if not a bang, at least an interesting, thought-provoking, or entertaining beginning.

In his book *First Paragraphs*, **Donald Newlove** describes story beginnings as "the first welling of life that gives breath to a piece of writing." Without that initial breath of life, many good stories never have a chance. The beginning of a story should grab the reader, invite her in, and compel her to read on.

I sat home one fall evening with a stack of student writing in front of me—third grade papers, 88 stories in all. The children had written these pieces in response to a 45-minute timed prompt. My job was to read and assess these papers, identify areas of need, and work with the classroom teachers on instructional strategies to meet those needs.

This is the prompt that the children responded to:

> You are walking along the beach and discover a mermaid.
> Describe the mermaid and write a story about your adventure.

I sat back with a cup of tea, put my feet up, and made myself comfortable. I picked up the first paper and began to read:

"One sunny day..."

In summary, the story began one sunny day with the main character waking up, getting dressed, having breakfast, begging mom to take her to the beach, calling a series of friends, and finally, two-and-a-half pages later, arriving at the beach. The story, with its two pages of extraneous background material, ran out of steam before we ever got to the "good part"—the part about the mermaid. By the time the author introduced the mermaid, it was obvious that she'd run out of time. The mermaid was *mentioned* and that was that. Three quarters of the writing led up to something that never really happened. I put the piece aside, disappointed that this well-intentioned writer never got around to what could have been an interesting tale.

I picked up the next story in my pile and began to read: "One hot summer day..."

A feeling of deja-vu crept up on me. Hadn't the last story begun in almost exactly the same way?

Hmmm...I put it aside and scanned the beginnings of the rest of the 88 stories. About 80% of the stories began with some version of "One sunny day..." There were, however, a few alternate story beginnings. These included:

"This story is about..."

"Hi, my name is _____"

"Once upon a time..."

The *good* news was that, without having read past the first line of any of the remaining 87 stories, I already had one lesson suggestion. These kids desperately needed to learn how to write an entertaining beginning!

How *Not* to Make a Good First Impression

Let's go back to the party parallel and look at the various first impressions that are turn-offs. Each one has a literary counterpart, which I will demonstrate using the mermaid prompt as the basis.

The Limp Handshake/Zero Eye Contact Introduction. This type of story beginning feels nebulous. The reader cannot get a feel for what the story will be about. It does not hold the reader's attention or entice the reader into the fictional world.

> It was a nice day to do something outside. I wondered what I could do, but couldn't think of anything around the house that seemed fun. I was feeling bored and asked my mother what I should do. She didn't have any ideas either.

Is there any clue that this story will be about meeting a mermaid? At best, the boredom that the author describes is passed along to the reader, who feels no compulsion at all to read on!

The Never-Ending Small Talk Introduction. I find that this is, perhaps, the most common introduction of choice by student authors. Children often feel a need to thoroughly define their fictional world and provide background on the events leading up to the crux of the story.

The problem is that, more often than not, they never get to the basis of the story because they've spent so much time and energy on extraneous details at the beginning.

> One bright sunny July day I woke up. I got dressed and went down for breakfast. Dad had made me waffles with syrup and bacon on the side. It was delicious. I thought it would be a fun day to go to the beach, so I asked Mom. She said fine, so I called Susan, but Susan had to go to the dentist. So I called Kate, and she couldn't go either. Mom said why don't I call Maggie, so I did. She said yes, so I got my towel and bucket and put them in the car. Mom made lunch and....

All of the details are realistic and accurate relative to a real-life situation, but none of them is entertaining or relevant to the mermaid story.

The Stick-to-the-Facts Introduction.
This no-nonsense approach is more suited to expository, nonfiction, or report writing (although it certainly wouldn't do much to hold the reader's attention even in the informational realm). The informational tone of this story opening sends a confusing message to the reader, who picked up the story expecting to be entertained.

> This story is about the day that I went to the beach and met a mermaid. I saw the mermaid and went up to her. We talked, etc., etc.

Don't tell the reader what the story will be about! Just tell the story! The reader should be drawn into the fictional world, not informed about it.

The Cliché Introduction.
The thing about clichés is that, after a while, they lose their impact. In the right setting or circumstance, they work. The cliché sets us up to expect something. If a writer begins with a cliché such as, "Once upon a time," the reader expects a fairytale or a folktale—a classic sort of story set in the long ago or far away. So what's wrong with using it in the following example?

> Once upon a time my mother brought me to the beach. We parked over near the hot dog stand and got out. I walked along until I saw something weird by the rocks. It was a mermaid!

The problem here is that "Once upon a time" is inconsistent with the modern-day setting of this story. Driving to the beach and parking near the hot dog stand hardly seem consistent with the expectation of the tale taking place long ago and far away.

The Tell-All-About-Me Introduction. The problem with the story beginning below is that the focus is off. The emphasis on Tiffany is misleading because the story focus is on meeting a mermaid.

> Hi, my name is Tiffany. I am eight years old and I live in Stratford, Connecticut. I have brown hair and green eyes. I have a dog and two cats who I love a lot. I am in third grade. I love the beach, which is why I am going to tell you about my adventure there last summer.

This child sees her personal history and preferences as relevant to the story. I would encourage her to include that information in an author's profile at the end of the story, not as a part of the story itself. Even in a first-person narrative, this kind of tag-on beginning does not flow smoothly into the story.

How to Make a Positive, Memorable First Impression

In writing, just as in social situations, a good first impression is made when the audience is drawn in and attracted to what is being said. A memorable introduction is one that is interesting and entertaining; often, a memorable introduction is one in which questions are raised and curiosity aroused. When this happens, the audience (or listener) will not vanish at the first opportunity. They'll stick around, dying to hear more.

To discover some of the devices that authors use to create effective beginnings, I turned to literature, to stories that children enjoy. I found several techniques that were used successfully over and over again. These included **action, dialogue, questions, thoughts/feelings, and sound effects.**

Dialogue

This is how E.B. White draws the reader into his classic novel, *Charlotte's Web*:

> "Where's Papa going with that ax?" said Fern to her mother as they were setting the table for breakfast. "Out to the hoghouse," replied Mrs. Arable. "Some pigs were born last night."

The author began with **dialogue** between the main character and her mother. Their brief conversation grabs your attention and raises **story questions**: Why in the world does Papa need an ax? What will he do to those newborn pigs? The reader just has to read on to find out for sure!

Action

Here's how Sid Fleischman began a chapter in his middle-grade novel, *The Whipping Boy*:

> Hold-Your-Nose-Billy popped a clove of garlic into his mouth, ground it between his yellow teeth and helped himself to a veal pie.

Fleischman's chapter begins with a character doing something memorable. The author uses **action** as the hook. The action also reveals what the character is like.

Question

Another great opening is the use of a **question**. Here's how award-winning author Avi uses this technique in his novel *Blue Heron*:

> What—Margaret Lavchek asked herself—was magic really for?

Again, in the space of a sentence, the author introduces a character and raises a question.

Thoughts

In *Something Upstairs*, Avi uses the main character's **thoughts** to draw us immediately into the head and heart of the main character:

> As far as Kenny Huldrof was concerned, Los Angeles, California, was perfect.

Thoughts and feelings

Suzy Kline also draws the reader in through the use of **thoughts and feelings**. This example is from her chapter book, *Herbie Jones and the Class Gift*:

> Herbie Jones hated indoor recess. Especially in June.

What reader wouldn't identify with those sentiments?

Sound Effects

And finally, the technique that student writers seem to enjoy emulating most often—the **sound effect**. In her Newbery-winning middle-grade novel, *Bridge to Terabithia*, Katherine Paterson opens with:

Ba-room, ba-room, baroom, baripity, baripity, barapity, barapity— Good. His dad had the pickup going. He could get up now.

Paterson *could* have said, "He heard the noisy truck;" instead, she has the reader get inside the main character's head and listen along.

As you read, you will become more and more aware of these techniques. The same techniques for attention grabbing beginnings—action, dialogue, questions, thoughts/feelings, and sound effects—are used in adult popular novels and short stories as well. That is not to say that there aren't other ways in which an author can effectively begin a story. As author Patricia Reilly Giff says, "You can get away with what you can get away with." For example, Barbara Park begins each of her highly successful *Junie B. Jones* chapter books like this:

"My name is Junie B. Jones. The B. stands for Beatrice. Except I don't like Beatrice. I just like B. and that's all."

Although at first glance this resembles the dreaded, *"Hi, my name is..."* kind of beginning, there is a difference: Park uses this opening to immediately reveal Junie B.'s quirky personality and unique voice in a way that is humorous and entertaining. But Park's technique is an exception. For teaching and learning purposes, having a menu of the more typical attention-grabbing beginnings is helpful.

Introducing Students to These Techniques

The day after I read the 88 mermaid stories, I brought them back to school with me and read the beginning of each aloud to the children.

"Children," I say, "I'm going to read you some story beginnings. You think about them, and ask yourselves whether or not any of them grab your attention."

"Are these from the stories we wrote?" asks Christopher eagerly.

"Yes," I answer. "Listen to see if you hear your story beginning."

I start reading the opening sentence or so of the 10 or 12 papers I've selected.

"One sunny day I had nothing to do..."

I read the next paper.

"*One hot day* I went to the beach..."

I continue.

"*One hot day* I decided to go out..."

"*One hot afternoon* I thought I'd go cool off..."

"*One summer day* I left to go to the beach..."

I use the inflection in my voice to emphasize the redundant *one sunny day* variation in each example. By the fifth or sixth, the children are teasing, imitating me in a sing-song kind of way—"*One* sunny day, *one* summer day, *one* hot day..."

I stop. "What's the matter?"

Matt doesn't bother to raise his hand. "Every single sentence began with *one* something or other. It's the same old thing over and over." The others nod their heads in agreement.

"Should I read some more?" I ask.

They consider for a moment. Amelia raises her hand. "Are there any different kinds of beginnings in there?" she asks, gesturing toward the pile of papers in my hand.

I nod and read a few of the others.

"This is a story about seeing a mermaid."

"I am going to tell you a story about..."

"Hi, my name is_____ [*I leave out the author's name*] and I'm writing a story about..."

A glazed look begins to creep across their faces.

"So," I ask, "which beginning really grabbed your attention? Which one were you dying to hear more about?"

Silence. A giggle.

"None of them," blurts Peter. "They're all pretty boring."

"Yes," I agree, "they *were* a bit boring. But you know what? I can show you the kinds of tricks authors use that can give those boring beginnings a jump start just like that!" I snap my fingers to emphasize the ease with which I believe they can improve their work. "Listen to this," I say.

A Menu of Story Beginnings

At that point, I pull out a pile of books—great books with snappy beginnings, some of which I've noted at the beginning of each chapter. In some cases I read only the very first sentence of the book; for others, the first paragraph or the riveting start of a new chapter. (In longer works, the opening of a chapter functions like the beginning by grabbing the reader's attention.) In every case, the children beg me to read on. The beginnings are <u>that</u> good. Then we discuss how the author managed to grab their attention. Their responses translate into the list of techniques—action, dialogue, a thought or feeling, a question, a sound effect. I list these on chart paper. I head the paper A MENU OF STORY BEGINNINGS.

Then we go back to the mermaid prompt. I write the following sentence on the board:

One sunny day I went to the beach and saw a mermaid.

"Okay," I say, "Help me rewrite this boring beginning. Let's start with an action. We'll put the main character (me) right there in the setting (the beach) doing something interesting."

They call out numerous suggestions and I pick one. I translate it into a sentence and write it on the board:

ACTION:

I dove into the ocean, kicked my feet in the cool water, stood up, and wiped the water from my face. I paused. Something strange near the rocks caught my eye.

We discuss how the action is appropriate and logical given the setting (beach), and we talk about the interesting story questions it raises: What caught my eye? What was strange about it?

I read the before-and-after versions back to back. The children unanimously agree that the action version is much more entertaining.

"Now wait a minute," I say. "We're not finished yet. We have a few more tricks to try out. How about dialogue? Who can think of an exclamation that the main character might come out with? Remember, put the character in the setting and imagine what he or she might say!"

After a few minutes of brainstorming we come up with this:

DIALOGUE:

"What a great day for the beach!" I yelled as I splashed in the waves.

The children agree that this is definitely better than the original, but a few feel that the story questions that arose from the previous revision were important and shouldn't be left out. I suggest adding another sentence, and our revision becomes:

"What a great day for the beach!" I yelled as I splashed in the waves. Suddenly I stopped. "What in the world is that over by the rocks?"

We continue in much the same way, using each of the techniques that were illustrated in the literary examples we listened to. From time to time we go back to these literary examples to help us formulate our revisions. Here are the other examples:

A THOUGHT, QUESTION, OR FEELING: (If you were at the beach, what might you be thinking or wondering?)

> *If only I could swim out to that sandbar, I thought. There's something very strange out there. Something I've never seen here at the beach before.*

A SOUND EFFECT: (What sounds might you hear at the beach?)

> *Kersplash! The waves crashed over me as I stood staring at the strange sight out on the jetty.*

After this I hand the mermaid stories back to the children and ask them to revise their story beginnings using one of these techniques. They get right to work on it, eager to change their boring "before" beginning to an entertaining "after." I circulate, reading samples of their work aloud, offering encouragement and praise. They can hardly wait to share their revisions with the class.

Where and When Does a Story Really Start?

Using an action, dialogue, thought, feeling, question, or sound effect is a great way to make a good first impression. But another important consideration involves where and when a story really begins. For example, in the mermaid story, does the story begin at home in the bedroom, waking up? Or does it begin at the beach?

In his book *Plot*, **Ansen Dibell** explains where and when a story should begin:

> The first thing to realize is that generally you're *not* going to begin at the beginning. Your story's start, the actual words that begin the narrative, will be a good way along in the progress of the events you're imagining.

Dibell goes on to explain that the Greeks (as translated by the Romans) referred to this as *in medias res*, which translates: *in the middle of things*. In other words, as I tell the children, your story should begin as close to the main event as possible. As soon as children have been exposed to the various ways they can begin their stories, I post this reminder about *when* their story should begin:

Begin your story as close to the main event as possible!

For example, if the story is about an adventure in a jungle, begin the story in the jungle at the first hint of danger, not at home packing your suitcase. If the story is about finding a buried treasure on a deserted island, begin by digging the hole under the palm tree, not by sitting around the kitchen table planning the trip a month before.

This is important for two reasons. First, in wading through all of that preliminary extraneous material, the reader is likely to tire. The second reason that this is important relates to timed prompts. If a student spends the majority of the allotted time working up to the main event, chances are she will never get around to what's really important.

I also post the following reminder for story beginnings:

State a <u>purpose</u> for your story action!

Children sometimes neglect to do this. Their ideas are very clear to them, and so they assume that the reader will understand what the story is about. If the tale is about a camping adventure, *tell* the reader you're going camping. If it's a story about exploring a haunted house, *tell* the reader what the main character's goal is. Don't assume they'll figure it out. This should be done early on in the story, within the first paragraph. Popular novelist **Phyllis Whitney** agrees:

> Probably the best way to start any story, long or short, is to show a character with a problem doing something interesting. The more quickly you can make what is happening clear, the more likely you'll be to draw your reader into your story.
> —Phyllis A. Whitney, *Guide to Fiction Writing*

What follows is the opening of eight-year-old Hanna's mermaid story, "The Wish." Her story beginning provides a good example of what I mean by stating a purpose for story action and what Phyllis Whitney means by making what is happening clear. Notice how Hanna begins with a sound effect, draws the reader immediately into the setting through the use of sensory information/description, and then sets a purpose for the story action (exploring at the beach).

> A sound! ↓   The Wish
>
> Woosh! Went the wind as my feet   Action! ↗
>
> touched the soft sand. I was   Setting a purpose!   exploring at the
>
> beach, and was having a great time.
>
> It was a beatiful day, the trees swayed in
>
> the wind, and the gulls soared through
>
> the sky.

WOOSH! Went the wind as my feet touched the soft sand. I was exploring at the beach and was having a great time. It was a beautiful day, the trees swayed in the wind, and the gulls soared through the sky.

The Opening Act, in Review

Imagine you're at a magic show, eagerly waiting to see the main event, the big name act—someone like, say, David Copperfield. But first you sit back to enjoy the opening act—some young up-and-coming talent slated to whet the audience's appetite, warm them up, and make them eager for what is to come.

A story beginning is a lot like a warm-up act. Both should grab your attention, get you excited, and create a feeling of anticipation. But it shouldn't take forever: If the opening is too long, the audience gets restless.

The opening act also makes a kind of a promise to the audience. If that promise is that the big-name magician will pull a rabbit from his hat, it had better happen! (And it better not be a guinea pig or a chinchilla!) Story openings also set a tone and make promises to readers. A tale that starts off with a dark, foreboding feeling needs to deliver a scary or mysterious story, not a happy, funny tale that made a 180-degree turn around, leaving the reader lost and confused. Give the audience what you've promised; that's the unwritten agreement.

Openings are an invitation. The use of action, dialogue, thoughts, feelings, questions, even sound effects invite the reader into the fictional world. But once the reader has accepted the invitation, the author still has a big challenge ahead: Keep the reader interested and entertained enough to stick with the story through to a satisfying ending! You needn't cast a spell on your audience to accomplish this! The remaining chapters on elaboration, suspense, main events, and satisfying endings are all the tricks you'll need!

Elaborating With Details

. . . .

or, Take a Picture, It Lasts Longer!

I stand before my second graders, hugging a photograph against my chest. They squirm, trying to get a look, but I keep the picture covered. I've got their attention now.

"What's that?" asks Alan

"Yeah, what is it? Let us see!" echoes the chorus.

I take a step back and clutch the picture closer.

"I have a picture here," I tell them. "But not just *any* picture."

I wait.

"What's it a picture of?" blurts out Michael.

"Come on, show us!" says Emma.

I pause. "Well," I say, "I'll tell you about it." I sneak a peek at the picture. "Here I have a picture of a neat, really awesome dog."

A wave of "oohs" and "ahhs" erupts from the children who are now leaning expectantly over their desks in anticipation of a glimpse of my neat, awesome dog.

"Show us!" they beg. "Come on, show us!"

"But I've already told you about it," I say, "it's neat and really awesome."

They begin to moan and groan. "What kind of dog? How big is it? Is it your own dog?"

I hold up one hand to silence them. "I'll show you the picture," I say, "but not yet." Their smiles turn to impatient pouts.

"I want you to *imagine* this neat, awesome dog. Go on," I urge. "Form a picture of him in your mind."

They close their eyes, imagining the canine of their dreams. While they're imagining, I distribute drawing paper.

"Okay," I tell them, "I want you to draw this neat, really awesome dog. When you're done, I'll show you the picture. Then we'll compare."

They eagerly set about this task, gathering crayons, trading markers. Laurel works on a fancy little Yorkie with a purple ribbon in its hair. Brian creates his version of a large, smiling golden retriever. Ellen draws a curly-haired black poodle with a diamond collar. T.J. and Drew argue about whose dog is better—T.J.'s polka-dotted Dalmatian or Drew's blue-eyed Siberian husky. As they work, they tell me details about their dogs. "See her long, silky ears?" asks Sarah. Robbie, pointing to his drawing adds, "They cut the boxer's tail off and leave this little stump."

"Okay, okay everyone," I call. "Now you can see my picture." They gather around, waving their drawings and arguing about whose dog my photo will most closely resemble.

"Tah-dah!" I say as I hold it up for display. There is a small wave of contention, disbelief, and laughter at the sight of the photo. Pictured is a small bug-eyed chihuahua decked out in a red and black beaded vest topped with a red sombrero trimmed in gold shiny thread.

Clay shakes his head. "You said the dog was neat and really awesome. This dog is..." He paused, considering. "Weird and puny."

Many nod their heads in agreement. But Dana disagrees. "I think he's neat. And his hat is awesome."

I nod, pleased with the way this conversation is going. "So," I ask, "What was the problem with my description?"

"You really didn't *tell* us anything," Robbie complains. "What you think is neat and awesome isn't the same thing as what I think." He emphasizes this statement with a disdainful nod toward my chihuahua.

Play "Imagine and Compare"

What follows is a discussion about general versus specific adjectives. Beforehand I'd scanned my Sears catalog and a variety of magazines for other pictures—a *fabulous* bedroom, a *really cute* baby, a *delicious* meal, a *gorgeous* dress. We play the "imagine, then look and compare" game with the rest of the pictures. The children soon see why general words like nice, pretty, cool, awesome, fantastic, great, cute, scary, and beautiful really mean very little. At best, they mean different things to different people.

"Can words ever paint accurate pictures?" I ask. The children look doubtful. I ask them to close their eyes again, listen, and imagine. I open Roald Dahl's book *The BFG*, flip to the section I want, and begin to read:

> In the moonlight Sophie caught a glimpse of an enormous long pale wrinkly face with the most enormous ears. The nose was sharp as a knife, and above the nose there were two bright flashing eyes, and the eyes were staring straight at Sophie. There was a fierce and devilish look about them.

I glance up from the book. They are mesmerized by the magic of Dahl's words. I look at them, biting my lower lip, one eyebrow raised and say, "The author *could* have just written, *Sophie saw a scary giant*."

"No," they protest, "that would be boring!" They beg me to read on. We discuss how the author enabled them to observe the scene through the main character's eyes. I explain, with great excitement, that I am going to teach them how to write that way.

That's how our journey into elaborative detail begins. And what a journey it will be!

The Journey Into Elaboration

Most children do not have a clear sense of *why* their stories need elaborative detail. They are also unsure about *when* and *how* to add details to their writing. So when their teachers, in response to sparse, general writing, urge children to add more details, the results are often disappointing. The kinds of details children typically add fall into the following categories:

Color. Students go through their story and insert color words for as many things as possible. *We walked across the* green *grass and looked up into the* blue *sky*. (Isn't the grass usually green? The sky blue? These are irrelevant details.) Or: *She wore a* red *shirt,* blue *pants, and* black *shoes*. (So what? Is this a police report or an entertaining story?)

Size. Same technique as for color, except now the characteristic is height and/or weight. *The big* 6 foot two inch two hundred pound *man came in*. (This is only relevant if the plot ties in to the man's large size.) Or: *She picked up the yellow*, six-inch *pencil*. (Does that detail add to the mood, tone, or entertainment value of the story?)

Generalities. Words like big, nice, pretty, cool, or scary can be interpreted in different ways by different readers.

Action. Many students confuse action with descriptive detail. When asked to add more details, they simply have the main character *do* more *stuff*. This contributes to rambling narratives that lack the focus of a single, meaningful main event.

Emphasis. This one is used when all else fails—The *big dog* becomes the <u>*very*</u> *big dog*. On the second revision it becomes the <u>*very*</u>, <u>*very*</u> *big dog*. And, to really drive home the point, the *VERY, VERY, VERY big dog*. Children *really, really, really* do this a lot. You get the idea.

A Grocery List. This is a favorite of children who have a good grasp of adjectives: They clump descriptive words together in a list. (*The big, cute, brown, furry, friendly, dog...*)

In order to expand children's repertoire of descriptive tools, I begin by raising w*hy, when, and how* questions about elaborative detail. The best way to begin is by studying and analyzing why authors create and use elaborative details.

Elaborative Detail: The Blood of Fiction

In *The Art of Fiction*, John Gardner says, "Vivid detail is the life blood of fiction." Specific detail enables the reader to experience and observe the fictional world through the main character's five senses. At its best, detail creates immediacy, a sense for the reader of "being there." This kind of elaboration is what writers refer to as **Show, Don't Tell.**

Here is an example of *telling:*

> *The storm was very bad at the shore.*

Here is an example of *showing:*

> Under the darkened sky, the sea was white, running sidewise, exploding in sheets of spray against the long arm of land that formed their end of the little bay.

> —from *The Eyes of the Amaryllis* by Natalie Babbitt

Children's author **Patricia Reilly Giff** calls this kind of description a "slice of life." Here is a slice of life from *The Great Gilly Hopkins* by Katherine Paterson:

> The couch was brown and squat with a pile of cushions covered in graying lace at the far end. A matching brown chair with worn arms slumped at the opposite side of the room. Gray lace curtains hung at the single window between them, and beside the window was a black table supporting an old time TV set with rabbit ears.

Instead of taking her readers along for a tour of the room and *showing* them each detail, Ms. Paterson could have just said, "The room looked shabby." That would have been "telling"—and not nearly as effective.

These examples clearly demonstrate *why* authors use elaborative detail. It is the stuff that breathes life into their stories. The *when* and *how*—when to use elaborative detail, and how to generate it effectively—are more complicated questions.

When to Use Elaborative Detail

As you can see from the examples at the beginning of this chapter, details added indiscriminately do not enhance a story. When should an author add elaborative detail?

Barry Lane, teacher and author, can help us out here. In his book *After the End*, he refers to a "magic camera" that can freeze a moment or a scene in time. This "snapshot," as Lane refers to it, is a written observation of that frozen moment in time. "Freezing the moment" is critical in the art of description. When an author describes, the action in the story stops.

Barry Lane's camera analogy is a powerful one for our purposes. We take a camera along to a memorable event to preserve highlights of the occasion. *Highlights* is the key word here. The following mini-lesson illustrates this point.

A Vacation Tale—How Much to Tell?

"Boys and girls," I say, "Come on over to the story corner. I want to tell you about my vacation to the Grand Canyon." The children, loving any personal story the teacher has to tell, flock to the cozy nook in the corner of the room. I wait until they're settled and until I have their undivided attention.

"We left the house at around 5:00 in the morning. We put the suitcases in the car and went to the airport. The car was gray, and our suitcases were this sort of flowery cloth material. It was a partly cloudy day, and since it was hot, I wore shorts and a tee shirt."

The children are already beginning to squirm. I go on, describing every extraneous detail of our ride to the airport, checking our bags, boarding the plane, eating our in-flight lunch, landing, collecting our baggage, renting a car, loading the luggage in the trunk.

At about this point, Daniel blurts, "Are we *ever* going to get to the Grand Canyon?" The others echo his sentiments.

I pause. "I did bring my photo album along. Would you like to see it?"

"Yes!" they exclaim.

I open the book and show them my photos, offering details about each. My collection of photos includes a shot of the resort we stayed at in Sedona, my family hiking the brilliant, majestic red rocks, an ancient abandoned Pueblo Village, numerous shots of us at the rim of the Grand Canyon, and shots of the wildlife, habitat, and gorgeous views of the region.

The children crowd in closer, eager for a better look. Finally I close the album. "If I wanted to write a personal experience story about my trip, what do you think I'd include?"

They all answer at once, each naming their favorite photograph. I stop them with a raised finger.

"Hey, wait a minute," I say. "Before I showed you these pictures, I told you a lot about my trip. Shouldn't I include any of that?"

They consider this for a moment. Cameron responds. "Well, you could mention how you got there. But the rest of that stuff was..." He pauses, a little uncomfortably. I know what he was about to say. I provide the word for him. "Boring?"

They nod, clearly afraid of hurting my feelings. I press on, unaffected. "Why are the photographs more interesting?"

"'Cause we can *see* them!" says Emily. They all agree.

"Well," I say, "what if I took photos of all the things I told you about—the car, the airport, the suitcases, my tee shirt..."

Allison rolls her eyes. "You wouldn't take pictures of all that, silly," she says. "You'd run out of film!"

Brian jumps in. "And why would you want a picture of your car or your suitcase in your vacation album?" They giggle at this idea.

"Exactly!" I say. "And writing a story is a lot like taking photographs. The author aims and focuses his magical writing camera only at the most interesting and exciting *characters, settings,* and *objects* in the story. The author brings these important things into focus and freezes those observations in time so that the reader can enjoy them as if he or she were actually there!"

Using Description Selectively

So *when* to use description? Description is typically used to highlight and draw the reader's attention to story-critical characters, settings, or objects. This prevents a "police blotter" report of extraneous details that muddy the waters and distract the reader.

When I conference with my students about their writing and come to a key character, setting, or object that interests me, I tell them how much I'd love to view a snapshot of it. Questions I ask about during conferencing regarding details or description include:

❖ If you could take four (or five, or whatever) photographs within this story, what would you MOST want your readers to see? (This is a means of generating relevant detail.)

❖ Does this description enhance the story and draw the reader in, or does it distract the reader from the main event?

❖ Would you use up a frame of film on this detail and display this "snapshot" in your story album? (This question is posed regarding extraneous or distracting details in a draft.)

I often practice deciding when to elaborate with detail and description by summarizing a familiar story for the children and asking them to respond with their invisible magical cameras. They aim their cameras at me as I speak. When I come to a "photo-op," they take a snapshot with a clicking sound and a pressing motion with their index fingers. It usually goes something like this:

"Once there was a little girl named Little Red Riding Hood (*CLICK/SNAP—story-critical character*). She lived with her mother in a house in the woods. She set out to bring her granny a basket of food. She walked through the deep dark forest (*CLICK/SNAP—story-critical setting*). Along the way she gathered flowers and hummed a little tune. As she wandered off the path, she met up with a big bad wolf (*CLICK/SNAP—story-critical character*)."

I follow this "photo-op" with some discussion questions:

❖ Why not take a snapshot of Red Riding Hood's Mother? *(Red's mother is NOT a story-critical character. Her appearance does not significantly affect the story.)*

❖ Why not take a snapshot of her house? *(Factors such as the color, style, and condition of her house are irrelevant.)*

❖ Why not take a snapshot of what's inside the lunch basket? *(It doesn't make a bit of difference to the outcome of the story. To focus attention on it misleads the reader into thinking that the specific food items will play an important part in the story.)*

In this way, children begin to recognize story-critical elements and emphasize them in such a way that their writing maintains focus and moves in a meaningful direction without descriptive distraction.

Using Questions to Generate Elaborative Detail

We know *why* authors use elaborative detail, and we've seen *when* they use it. However, without knowing techniques and skills for effectively generating elaborative detail, the *why* and *when* become irrelevant. So exactly *how* do we instruct students to expand and enhance their writing in this way?

The answer is through the use of questions. The answers to questions about key characters, settings, or objects in a story provide useful elaborative material.

To introduce this technique, I tell the children that they are going to help me write a description of a story-critical object—for example, a crown. I begin by setting the stage with a quick story summary.

"Boys and girls, listen to this story summary. I was exploring a cave in the woods and made an amazing discovery. Sitting on a pedestal, with a mysterious light shining down on it, was a royal crown!"

I go on to tell them that I want to write a description of this crown, and I want them to help me. I ask them to think about the attributes or characteristics the crown might have in each of the following categories. I list the categories on the board to help them form a mental image:

color	size	material	age
texture	condition	shape	weight

Next, I ask questions and record the class's responses.

❖ **What color was the crown?** (*gold with red jewels and green crystals*)

❖ **What size was it?** (*It was big, suited to a very large man or a person with lots of hair.*)

❖ **What material was it made out of?** (*gold*)

❖ **How old was it?** (*hundreds of years old*)

❖ **What was the texture?** (*The band was smooth, and the points standing up around the edge were bumpy.*)

❖ **What condition was it in?** (*There were many dents and scratches on it.*)

❖ **What shape was it?** (*circular with triangular points*)

❖ **How much did it weigh?** (*about four pounds*)

And another revealing question that generates interesting detail:

❖ **What did it remind you of?** (*something King Arthur would have worn*)

First, I read off the attributes, grocery-list style:

"The crown was gold with red jewels, green crystals, was large, old, smooth and bumpy, dented and scratched, circular with triangular points, and reminded me of something King Arthur would have worn."

The children object to the list, knowing instinctively that it "doesn't sound right." This provides the perfect opportunity to revise the listed attributes into a series of sentences.

I write these details on the board in complete sentences, with no more than one or two details per sentence, in paragraph form. I always begin with a sentence that states the subject of our "snapshot."

There, sitting on a wooden pedestal, shining in the mysterious beam of light, sat an amazing crown. It was gold with red jewels around the rim and green crystals at the tip of each point. It was large and probably belonged to a very large man with a lot of hair. It was made of gold. It was probably hundreds of years old. It was smooth around the edge. It was bumpy along the points. It was worn out and scratched with many dents. It was made of a smooth circular band that fit around the head and tall points that stood up around the rim. It weighed about four pounds. It reminded me of something King Arthur would have worn.

Sentence Starters: Encouraging Variety

Notice that I purposely began each sentence in the above example with some variation of *it*. When I read the paragraph aloud to the children, I really use the inflection in my voice to emphasize the repetitious "it was." The children recognize immediately that, while the details are interesting, the sentences sound redundant because each one begins the same way. This leads us directly into the next step.

I revise the story for them again, this time focusing on sentence variety:

There, sitting on a wooden pedestal, shining in the mysterious beam of light, sat an amazing crown. My eye was drawn to the red jewels around the rim and green crystals at the tip of each point. The large crown must have belonged to a big man with a lot of hair. The golden finish glimmered in the light, and I shivered when I realized what it must be worth. I supposed that it must be very old—hundreds of years old, at least. As I ran my hand along the rim, I was surprised at its smooth finish, but the points felt as bumpy and rough as the arms of a starfish. The bumps, dents, and scratches all over the crown made me think it had been through many battles. I lifted it off the pedestal and was surprised at how heavy it was. Perhaps long ago it had belonged to King Arthur himself!

We compare the before-and-after versions of this description, reading each aloud. I begin a chart of "sentence starters" to encourage sentence variety, and we add to it as the year goes on. Children often use this "menu of choices" when they get stuck.

The chart looks something like this:

SENTENCE STARTERS

It was _____ .
I noticed _____ .
I supposed that _____ .
As I ran my hand along it _____ .
I was surprised by _____ .
It felt like _____ .
The _____ was _____ .
I loved the way _____ .
It reminded me of _____ .

After modeling an example I have students repeat the process and create their own paragraphs on a separate, but related, theme. I circulate and help them with sentence variety and sequencing, if necessary. Most—with a reminder about avoiding "grocery lists" and redundant "broken record" sentence beginnings—do quite well writing a fairly cohesive, interesting paragraph. I read examples of their creative work aloud, thus encouraging others. Sometimes I will provide students with relevant questions for them to answer. (See example, next page.)

During this guided practice, students love to listen to each other's work and often "borrow" ideas. In my class one student described an old woman's nose as being "sharp as a dagger." The rest of the class enjoyed the simile so much that similar examples crept into their writing as well. This kind of "borrowing" is extremely valuable and is practiced by experienced authors all the time.

Here is the lesson sequence I use for teaching elaboration:

1. Teacher provides a story summary and topic sentence.
2. Teacher and class generate questions about a story critical character, setting, or object.
3. Class brainstorms answers.
4. Teacher models transforming answers into complete sentences, in paragraph form.
5. Teacher models paragraph revision using sentence variety.
6. Teacher provides guided practice opportunities for children to work through the same process on a related topic.

I repeat this sequence over and over again throughout the school year, changing the topic so that children can experience the techniques with a variety of characters, settings, and objects. Eventually students will internalize their questions and generate the details directly into their writing.

Here are some examples of alternate topics for this lesson sequence along with sample topic sentences and detail-generating questions. Notice that the nature of the questions changes based on the topic.

Topic sentence regarding a setting

I couldn't believe how beautiful the desert was!

Possible questions
- What color was the sky?
- What kinds of plants did you see?
- What was the weather like?
- Were there any animals around?
- What did you hear there?
- What did you feel there?

(We use this exercise when we are reading about the desert habitat in science.)

Topic sentence regarding a character

An incredible giant stood before me!

Possible questions
- How big was he?
- What color hair/eyes did he have?
- What size/shape were his nose, ears?
- How old did he look?
- What kind of expression was on his face?
- What was he wearing?

(We use this exercise when reading Roald Dahl's The BFG.*)*

Topic sentence regarding a character/animal

The frog stared at me from the lily pad!

Possible questions
- What color was it?
- How big was it?
- What was its texture?
- What kind of eyes/legs/feet did it have?
- What kind of expression was on its face?
- What kind of sound did it make?

(We use this exercise when studying and reading about frogs and toads.)

Integrating these writing exercises into the curriculum in this way is advantageous for many reasons. First of all, students come to the writing task with sufficient background knowledge and interest; conversely, drawing upon their knowledge during the writing task reinforces and supports prior learning.

Connecting elaborative writing to related art projects is another valuable learning experience. For example, before we work on the descriptive piece on the giant, I distribute sheets of long, narrow construction paper and ask them to draw their giant. This helps children who benefit from visual cues, and after their writing is completed, proofread for spelling, capitalization and punctuation, and copied over, we combine their construction paper giants with their written pieces for an outstanding bulletin board.

What can you expect from students when these techniques are employed? Here are some examples of elaborative detail written by second and third grade students:

I was at my grandmother's house last Thanksgiving. One of my cousins and I went up into the attic to explore. The stairs going up were very narrow and creaky. The attic was dark and spooky. It was filled with cobwebs, and rat and mouse droppings were scattered on the floor. There was of course that old musty smell of something old or dead. We couldn't reach the light switch so the only light came from a small window.
                                                    —Gordon Verrill, age 8

It was a Siamese cat! She was the size of two of her kind put together. She had hideous sharp teeth that hung from her mouth. The color of her fur was black, as dark as night and white as a fresh marshmallow.
                                                    —Jessica Matis, age 8

I gasped! I couldn't believe what was in my way. My mouth hung open. I almost fainted when I saw how tall he was. His ears were as big as a rhinoceros. Blue rags dangled from his huge shoulders. His face was covered in wrinkles like a prune. His eyes were as big as watermelons. I stared for what seemed like hours. Then I noticed he was a giant!
                                                    —Annie Wiswell, age 8

In this last example, notice the way Annie *shows* how she was feeling when she encountered the giant. As Annie demonstrates, another important descriptive tool in writing has to do with the main character's thoughts and feelings.

Thought, Emotion, Description

When an author "shows" rather than "tells" how a character is thinking or feeling, the results are much more powerful and memorable. For example, I could write:

Alex was furious. *(That's telling.)*

Or I could show what *furious* looks, sounds, and feels like:

Alex's face turned a deep shade of red. His jaw was clenched, and his hands were curled into tight fists. He glared out through squinty eyes and breathed heavily. The veins in his neck seemed about ready to pop. *(That's showing!)*

How can you teach this technique to students? I enjoy a bit of play-acting as a means of introducing this skill in a memorable, entertaining way.

"Looking at" Feelings

I walk into the hall outside my classroom for a moment or two, come back in, and excitedly close the door behind me.

"Wait 'til you hear this!" I say.

The children crowd around me.

"I just saw Miss Andren *(a teacher they all know)* out there in the hallway! She was *so* excited!"

"What happened?" they ask.

"I don't know," I reply.

"What did she say?" asks Amelia.

"Nothing," I reply.

"Then how do you know she was excited?" asks Michael.

"I could tell just by looking at her," I explain. "Her hands were clasped in front of her like this." I demonstrate for them. "Her eyes were open very wide, and she had a big smile on her face."

They are nodding and getting visibly excited as I add more energy to my description.

"And she jumped up and down, up and down, making these funny little ooh-ooh sounds!"

"So, what was she so excited about?" Emma asks.

"I don't really know," I explain. "I didn't have time to ask her." *(I usually warn Miss Andren first, so that she's prepared for the hundred or so questions she'll be faced with. She usually explains that she was incredibly excited to hear what great writers they're becoming!)*

A hand-drawn chart titled "Excited":

> **Excited**
> - A big smile on your Face.
> - You're runing arownd like crazy!
> - Your jumping up and down.
> - Throwing a millon dollars up in the air.
> - Your hair is sticking up lik rokets
> - Your eyes pop out

I follow this up with a discussion about what feelings look like. I write each emotion or feeling on a separate sheet of chart paper or poster board. These include:

angry	sad	happy	excited	embarrassed	shy
nervous	tired	cold	hot	afraid	shocked

We look at one or two of these together, let's say "afraid" and "hot." The children tell me what these feelings *look* like, and I chart their responses. After modeling one or two examples, I divide the class into cooperative groups and have each group tackle one or two different feeling charts. When done, each group reads what their feeling looks like (without naming it), and the class guesses it. They must listen to the entire list before guessing because many of the "clues" are indicators of more than one feeling. Collectively these "clues" begin to point to a specific emotion or feeling. This realization encourages children to write three or four sentences when using this skill in their writing. Charts look something like this:

AFRAID Hands shaking Knees like rubber Covering mouth with hand Breathing fast Biting nails Whimpering	**HOT** Red in face Sweat on face, back Fanning self with hand Moving slowly Yawning	**SAD** Tears in eyes Trembling lips Hanging head Shoulders drooped Frown Dragging feet Crying
NERVOUS Hands shaking Biting bottom lip Butterflies in stomach Stuttering Swallowing hard	**HAPPY** Smiling Face Eyes open wide Clasping hands together Jumping up and down Laughing	**COLD** Shivering Rubbing hands together Hugging self Blowing on hands Seeing vapors of breath
SHY Blushing Looking down Speaking softly Arms crossed Standing back from the group	**SHOCKED** Mouth wide open Eyes popping open Hand covering mouth Gasping Stepping back	**TIRED** Droopy eyes Yawning Stretching Slouching Rubbing eyes
ANGRY Red in the face Hands on hips Glaring Hands in fists Jaw clenched Veins popping	**EMBARRASSED** Blushing Hanging head Holding back tears Rolling eyes Stomach flips Hiding face	**EXCITED** Mouth wide open Heart pounding Eyes wide open Hands clasped Jumping Clapping

All of our charts are left hanging up throughout the year for student reference.

When conferencing with students on their stories, I look for critical points where their character is feeling strong emotions. I'll ask:

How is this character feeling at this point?
What might that feeling look like?

Then they write down their responses (at least three or four sentences) using good sentence variety.

Revising Using Before-and-After Books

It is clear that adding elaborative detail to a piece of writing enhances it greatly. In a first draft a student might write a general statement ("The room was messy") and later, after our conference, *show* rather than tell:

The floor was covered with wrinkled clothes. Toys were scattered everywhere. It was impossible to find a place to sit because of the piles of papers and laundry on the sofa and chairs.

One way to encourage this kind of revision is by turning a composition book into a Before-and-After Book. My students use these at least once or twice a week.

I distribute strips of paper printed with general statements for them to extend through revision. Children paste these strips on a **Before** page and write their revision on the facing **After** page.

Here is an example of a second grader's **Before** and **After** revision. Notice the way she shows the character's feelings and draws the reader in through the use of the five senses.

Before

A SNAPSHOT is a descriptive section of a story. A snapshot STOPS THE STORY ACTION and describes, using the 5 senses. Snapshots make the story interesting and fun to read. Read this general BORING sentence:

The Snow Monster stood before me.

Write a snapshot of the snow monster. Answer these questions. Use interesting words and good sentence variety!

How big is it?   What kind of fur/hair does it have?
Tell about the size and shape of its body.
What kind of eyes does it have?
What kind of ears does it have?
What kind of snout/nose does it have?
What kind of mouth/teeth? What kind of expression?
What kind of sound does it make?
Tell about its arms, legs, claws.
How did it move?
How did you feel when you met this beast?

After

The snow monster stood before me. He was huge! I saw that he was made out of frostey, white snow that covered his whole body. His round head was very cold and very wet. He had black eyes that squinted in the moonlight. His nose was frozen and stiff. His mouth opened and I saw his teeth that glistened in the moonlight. He stuck his tongue out and said, "Bllaaaaa!" He opened his arms wide and started to walk toward me with his long legs. His movement was very slow and very quiet. I screamed, I was so scared! I gulped and my heart pounded.

A variation of this is to have students paste a sparse, general statement from one of their own stories on a left hand blank page and label it **Before**. On the facing page, they paste their detailed revision and label it **After**.

Children read their Before-and-After pieces to the class, and their efforts are met with applause and praise from their peers. Suddenly they become proud of the obvious differences between their **Before** and **After** versions. Because of this, "revision" takes on a much more positive connotation for them.

The Magic of Elaboration

By exploring the activities in this chapter, you and your and students will find that you suddenly have quite a few elaborative "tricks" up your sleeves!

You can suggest specific, rather than general ways in which your students can add descriptive detail ("I'd love to see a snapshot of that!" or "Can you show this, rather than tell it?" or "What would that feeling look like?"), and students will have the skills necessary to accomplish it. Students will be able to recognize general versus specific detail, identify where to add relevant details (a story-critical setting, character, or object), understand and use questioning techniques for generating vivid description, create interesting, varied sentences, and understand and experience the benefits of revision.

And, most important, as students learn how to conjure up words to convey strong images and deep feelings, something really magical happens—they begin to view themselves as *writers!*

CHAPTER 5

Developing Suspense

. . . .

or, Slowly I Turn, Step by Step . . .

Suddenly she froze. There was something coming up the street on the opposite side. It was something black... Something tall and black... Something very tall and very black and very thin.   —*The BFG* by Roald Dahl

Wary, she crept forward. The closer she came to the log, the stronger grew a scent unfamiliar to her. She sensed trouble. She was still sniffing when she heard the sound of a twig snapping behind her. She spun about and gasped.

—*Poppy* by Avi

Suspense—that nail-nibbling, edge-of-your-chair kind of magic that compels the reader to turn the page, finish the chapter, and devour the book! Could you have easily put the book down after reading either of the suspenseful paragraphs above?

Human beings are curious by nature. Most of us are intrigued by a mystery, titillated by a snippet of gossip, drawn to perplexing, unexplained phenomena. Such is the stuff of suspense. The skillful writer uses this to great advantage. R.L. Stine, author of the *Goosebumps* series, has parlayed suspense into a mega-successful empire that inspires even the most reluctant reader to pick up a book and dive right in.

So What Exactly Is Suspense?

My Funk and Wagnall's Standard Desk Dictionary defines suspense as follows:

1. The state of being uncertain, undecided, or insecure, usually accompanied by anxiety, apprehension, etc.
2. An uncertain or doubtful situation

In order to build suspense, then, the author must create some uncertainty, anxiety, doubt, and apprehension. What the dictionary doesn't tell us is how difficult this can be! The author already knows what is going to happen, who is behind the door, what is making the spooky sound, and to whom the mysterious footsteps belong. The trick is not to give it away too soon!

The author must deliberately hold back in order to create the kind of tension that propels the readers into the thick of things and hooks them emotionally. Make the reader wait—but don't bore them—and tease your audience with just a little hint of what is going to happen. Make the reader wonder and worry along with the main character. Raise questions that the reader will want to have answered. In this way, the author holds the reader's interest, creates empathy for the main character, and moves the plot and story energy toward some significant main event.

What the Experts Say About Suspense

- ◆ In *Plot*, **Ansen Dibell** says that *waiting* to find out is what builds suspense.
- ◆ In *Guide to Writing Fiction*, **Phyliss Whitney** says, "Keeping curiosity high by dangling a carrot in front of the reader is the way to [create suspense], though this can be tricky to manage."
- ◆ In her book *A Sense of Wonder*, Newbery-winner **Katherine Paterson** quotes Charles Dickens as saying, "You must make them laugh, make them weep, but above all, make them wait!"

So how can students learn to do this—to tease the reader, put off the inevitable, dangle the carrot, create worry, raise questions, and snag the reader with a suspenseful hook? What techniques can add this magical tension to their writing?

Before they can learn how to *create* suspense, children must be able to recognize it and understand its function within a piece of writing. The best way to accomplish this is to expose them to examples of suspense in literature that they enjoy.

Here's how I introduce my second graders to the thrill and magic of suspense and leave them begging for more:

We gather in the library corner, and I open a book to read. We have been working on a theme in our reading anthology called Gifts and Treasures. As an extension of this, we've read numerous books about pirates, tall ships, and buried treasure. Today they are eager to hear the new story I've chosen—Jon Scieszka's chapter book titled *Not So Jolly Roger*. They wiggle for a moment or two in anticipation, but as I begin reading, the words seem to mesmerize them.

I read them the first 17 pages that tell, in a rollicking, fast-paced style, how three boys called The Time Warp Trio are transported back through time and find themselves in a coconut tree on a deserted island. They watch in horror as a pirate ship drops anchor and a band of nasty pirates comes ashore. The pirates begin digging for buried treasure beneath the very tree where the boys are perched. When one boy accidentally drops his baseball cap, they are discovered by the pirate leader. Here is the cliff-hanging paragraph I end with:

> He froze. He looked at the hat. Then he looked slowly up, up, up the trunk of my
> tree. Our eyes met and my heart went as numb as my foot. The black pirate
> growled, "Arrrrrrrgh," and grinned a crazy smile. I swear I saw his eyes flashing
> red. Then he pulled out two pistols, aimed, and fired.

I pause and make a big show of closing the book. A collective howl of protest goes up from the group—"No! Don't stop now! Read us some more!" Lauren, one of my more dramatic youngsters, moans, "You're *so* mean to us!"

It is precisely the response I had anticipated. I sit back. "We'll read some more tomorrow," I assure them. But they will not be placated.

"Ohh....Come *on!*" they say in their whiniest voices.
"Why do you want me to read on?" I ask.
"We've *got* to find out what happens next!" says Tim, huffy and impatient.
"What is it you're wondering about?" I ask.
They bombard me with questions:
"What will the pirates do to them?"
"How will they escape?"
"Do they go forward in time to get away?"
"Do they actually get shot?"
"Is the head pirate really Blackbeard?"
"Will the boys share in the treasure?"
"Well," I say. "Our author, Jon Scieszka, has certainly done his job here. He's got you

right where he wants you!"

"What do you mean?" they ask. "Where has he got us?"

"He's got you *dying* to read on," I tell them. "The author has used *suspense*. It's the SUSPENSE that makes you wonder, worry, and ask questions!"

By now they're fidgeting like mad.

"Okay," says Clay, exasperation creeping into his voice, "You're right. We *are* dying to read on. So, let's keep on reading!"

As a matter of fact, the author has done such a good job of creating suspense that I have no choice but to read on. So I do, at least until the immediate tension is relieved. But when I stop, mark the page, and close the book (while their enthusiasm is still running high), I move right into a how-to lesson on building suspense. They can hardly wait. Thanks to Jon Scieszka, I've got them right where I want them!

Three Techniques for Suspense Building

RAISING STORY QUESTIONS

One of the easiest and most effective ways to build a sense of suspense or anticipation is by raising story questions. This can be done in a number of ways, all of which involve "getting inside" the main character's head and viewing the story situation from that character's point of view. This enables the reader to wonder and worry along with the main character.

Here's an example of stating a question that the main character is wondering about:

What was that noise? Was it just the wind or was it something...or someone else?

The same thing can be done with dialogue:

"What was that noise?" he whispered. Was it just the wind or was it something..., or someone, else?

It can also be done with a statement of concern, wonder, or worry:

"I wonder if that noise is just the sound of the shutters banging against the house."

A statement of hope with an undercurrent of worry and foreshadowing of a problem also works:

"I hope that noise isn't a ghost," she whispered.

WORD REFERENTS

Another way of raising story questions is through the use of word referents—words that stand for other words. This technique teases the reader by holding back some piece of critical information. The reader reads on to discover the missing piece.

Here is an example of a passage that uses this technique:

*Daniel froze. **It** loomed over him, at least seven feet of matted brown fur. **It** snarled and swatted at him with heavy, powerful claws. Daniel stared, horrified at **its** yellowed teeth visible behind its curled-back snout. **The beast** came closer and closer to him and Daniel backed up, afraid to turn his back for even a second.*

The reader wonders, "WHAT IS **IT**?" The author has given away plenty of hints, but never identifies the beast. Student authors often cut right to the chase, so to speak, using a statement such as *Daniel saw the mean bear.* Notice how much more entertaining the passage is than the statement above.

The referent need not be a pronoun—it can be another, more general word, such as "beast" in the example. The reader wonders, "What kind of beast?" Even when the clues are fairly obvious, readers get a certain satisfaction out of discovering later that their "guesses" or inferences were correct.

Can students master this technique? See what a terrific job eight-year-old Michael did using word referents for suspense building in his story.

1

Michael B. 2M The Desert Coyote
I zipped up the door of my
tent. I plopped down on my p
next to my friend, Clay. I w
camping out in the desert. Th
air was making me feel warm.
I started to play around wi
my zipper to my sleeping bag
~~...~~ I heard a
howling noise. I got up to s
what it was. I unzipped the
door and walked outside into
sandy desert. It still howled
I ran over to the noise. Just

2

Michael B. 2M
I saw a shadow on a hill. It
walked into the light of the
moon. The thing had brown fur
with a little mixture of dark red. It
down the hill. I hid behind t
bushes. Suddenly, I saw glowing
eyes staring straight at me. I
froze. My heart beat a little
faster. I felt a shiver down
spine. The eyes were golden an
the pupils were as blue as the
sky. I ran back towards the
The thing was running after

3

Michael B. 2M The desert coyot
It was a coyote! I ran faster.
The spikes of a dark green
cactus almost pricked me. I
looked back. It was getting
closer! I tried to think of something.
I got an Idea. I bent down
still running. I grabbed a huge
pile of warm sand from the sandy ground.
I threw it behind me and looked
back. The sand was a tall as the
coyote's paw. The coyote tripped
l over the sand. It seemed
The sand
hardened. The coyote was

4

Michael B. 2M
hart. I felt scared thinking
about the glowing eyes. I
rembered the dark shadow of the
coyote. And I decided to not go
camping away from home again.

THE MAGIC-OF-THREE

The Magic-of-Three is an age-old literary convention—suspense being just one applications. For example, take the Three Little Pigs: Would the story work if the *first* Pig had been sensible and clever, and the other two had failed? Or would Goldilocks and the *Nine* Bears be as satisfying as Mama, Papa, and Baby?

Of course by now you can see that it's no coincidence that Cinderella had **three** wicked stepsisters, that Dorothy, of Oz fame, met **three** friends on the way, that there are a **trio** of Billy Goats Gruff, and that a genie or fairy godmother grants not one, not 22, not 104, but **three** wishes.

As a suspense-building technique, the Magic-of-Three sets up a series of three hints which lead to a discovery. The plot follows this basic pattern:

The First Hint. The main character detects something amiss. Perhaps she hears a noise or sees something out of the corner of her eye. The hint might be visual or auditory, or it might involve any of the five senses. Nothing is discovered. The main character *reacts.* (Probably dismisses the hint as just her imagination.)

The Second Hint. The main character detects another hint, either something different or a similar hint of greater intensity. Again, nothing is discovered. The main character exhibits a more intense *reaction.*

The Third Hint. The main character detects a third hint, this one leading to a *discovery or revelation.*

> (1) Katie's Rainbow Adventure
> "I wonder what is down here," I asked myself as I tip-toed down the creaky stairs to my Grandma's basement. When I got down to the bottom of the stairs I was shocked. My eyes popped open and my mouth dropped down to the floor! Cobwebs were everywhere. A humongous trampoline almost filled the whole basement. Boxes were piled up to the ceiling.

Student writers love using this technique. Read eight-year-old Katie's process piece about a leprechaun, "Katie's Rainbow Adventure" (page 71). Notice her effective use of the Magic-of-Three.

What's the Magic Formula for Teaching Suspense?

1. **DEFINE** the skill by reading examples to the class.
2. **MODEL** the skill for the students by starting with a boring, give-it-away-too-soon example and revising it using each technique.
3. Provide **GUIDED PRACTICE** so students can try it on their own.

Using the *Define—Model—Guided Practice* Formula

After you've used literature to **DEFINE** suspense and the various techniques for implementing it, gather your students around. On top of a piece of chart paper, write:

Jan heard a weird noise and found a ghost in the closet.

Point out that the author gave this exciting discovery away too soon! Explain that you will be revising it, raising story questions, and stretching it out, and that you will **MODEL** how this is done. Ask questions such as, "What is your main character *wondering* about? What is she *worrying* about?" Write in their responses.

Jan wondered what the strange noises were coming from the closet.

Jan stood before the closet door worrying. What in the world could be making such a racket in there?

Next, encourage them to "slow down the action" and stretch out the act of Jan opening the closet door. Ask questions such as, *How would Jan go about opening the door—quickly or slowly? Would she be hesitant? How was she feeling at that moment, and what would those feelings look like? Did she hear anything as she opened the door?*

Here's how the paragraph might read with the action slowed down:

Jan reached for the knob with shaking hands. Her heart raced in her chest as she slowly turned the knob. The shuffling sounds seemed to be getting louder. She took a deep breath and threw open the door. She gasped! A filmy white ghost hovered before her!

Always, *always* ask, *Which example is more exciting, more entertaining? The "before" or the "after" version?* In my experience, students unanimously agree that their revised, new-and-improved version is by far better!

Then refer to the "before" version again, and explain that they'll have a chance to **PRACTICE** this by completing their own revision. At first you might worry that they will simply copy what you wrote when you modeled for them. I have never found this to be the case. You will be amazed at the creative variations they come up with. Walk around as they write, sharing terrific examples.

Teaching the Magic-of-Three

To teach the Magic-of-Three, repeat the **DEFINE—MODEL—PRACTICE** formula.

Begin by writing the "discovery" or "revelation" on chart paper:

Glenn saw a tiger on the jungle path.

Now explain that, instead of simply telling what Glenn saw, they will lead up to it using three hints. Begin by having them imagine Glenn in the middle of the jungle. (Put the character in the setting doing something.) Write down something like this:

Glenn walked through the deep jungle, peering into the underbrush.

If there was a tiger nearby, what hint might Glenn hear, see, or sense? Perhaps a rustling in the bushes, the snapping of a twig, a low-pitched growl, a flash of gold, or maybe even a feeling of being watched. Ask students for their suggestions. **MODEL** this process for them by translating these into the Magic-of-Three pattern. The end result might look like this:

> Glenn walked through the deep jungle, peering into the underbrush. A rustling sound off to the side of him stopped him in his tracks. Glenn turned and listened harder, but all was quiet. Perhaps it was only a bird or small animal nearby. He shrugged and went on. The snapping of a twig behind him sent chills up his spine. This was no bird and certainly not a small animal. Glenn spun around, ready to face whatever was out there. But there was nothing. His heart began to race, and he moved forward, more quickly this time. He started to sweat and concentrated on moving ahead, putting one foot in front of the other. That's when he saw them—a pair of golden, glowing eyes staring at him from the underbrush. Glenn froze as he realized that he was staring into the eyes of a huge Bengali tiger!

After comparing the "before" and "after" versions, allow the children to **PRACTICE** this skill on their own. Write this formula on the board to help them:

HINT 1—No discovery/reaction
HINT 2—No discovery/bigger reaction
HINT 3—DISCOVERY

You might encourage them to substitute themselves for Glenn and write their suspenseful passage in first person. Have them use a variety of hints. Circulate, read aloud, and offer plenty of encouragement.

A Lesson on Word Referents

Here's a great art-related idea for teaching the use of **word referents** for suspense building. It can be adapted to almost any theme or topic you choose.

Begin by choosing a topic such as the jungle walk in the previous example. Ask children to choose their own scary jungle creature but keep their choices secret! Distribute paper and have children draw a detailed picture of their beast. (Have some resource books on hand to help students with their drawings.) Be sure to remind them not to show anyone their animals!

When finished, have them write a description of their animal. (Use questioning techniques and sentence starters to help them generate good detail.) **(The difference here is to remind them that they must use word referents instead of the name of their beast!)** When they're done, give them each a large piece of paper that they can decorate with jungle trees, vines, and underbrush. Attach their word-referent description to this side of their paper—all of it except the revelation of what their creature is. Their piece should end with, "It was a...." On the back of the paper, they should attach their animal picture. Here is how their piece (on the jungle side of the paper) might read:

> *It was huge—the size of a truck. Its thick, leathery skin seemed to be wrapped around its body in heavy folds. The creature's four thick legs supported its weight like giant tree stumps. I stared into its small, marble-like eyes and shivered at the sight of the fierce curved horn that grew from the middle of its wide snout. It was a...*

Turning the page over reveals a drawing and the name of the creature, in this case a rhinoceros.

The finished projects can be read aloud as a guessing game or hung collectively as a bulletin board!

Projects for Teaching Word Referents

Try coming up with different art-related projects for teaching word referents. Here are a couple of suggestions to get you started:

The Pet in My Pocket. Students construct an envelope-style pocket into which they insert an illustration of their favorite pet. Their word-referent suspense piece is pasted to the outside.

Who's Behind the Door? Students make a paper flap door on a large piece of construction paper. Behind the door they draw a Halloween character. They attach a word-referent description of their character on the outside of the door. Open the door to reveal the character!

Katie's Rainbow Adventure

"I wonder what is down here?" I asked myself as I tiptoed down the creaky stairs to my grandma's basement. When I got down to the bottom of the stairs, I was shocked. My eyes popped open, and my mouth dropped to the floor! Cobwebs were everywhere. A humongous trampoline almost filled the whole basement. Boxes were piled up to the ceiling. "Teeheehee!" "What was that?" I said as I walked over to the other side of the basement. There was nothing there. My heart started to beat faster and faster. Cling! Cling! I heard two gold coins drop behind me. I took a big gulp and looked up. Nothing was there. I felt a tap on my shoulder. I turned around. There it was...a small, green thing. He had tiny glasses that didn't even fit him because they were too big for him. His round nose was as red as a cherry. I noticed that his clothes were all different shades of green. It was a leprechaun! My mouth dropped open and I stepped back. "Come on, we got a rainbow to catch," said the leprechaun as he took my hand and soared out the window. And then I knew I was on a red, orange, yellow, blue, purple, and green rainbow. I saw two beautiful blue birds sitting on a tree below. People looked like ants from all the way up there. A soft breeze swept across my face. We were so high that I could touch the sky! The rainbow reminded me of a giant lollipop. "Hold on to your panty hose, we're going down!" he said. Then I knew I was in a humongous pot of...of...GOLD!!! "Do I get to keep the gold?" I asked. "Of course you get to keep the gold," he said as he snapped his fingers together. Just then I was back at my Grandma's house again. I'll never forget the time when I fell into a big pot of gold. I'm glad that I have a giant pot of gold sitting right next to me!

"Magic of three section"

note use of word referents

After the Revelation

Suspense building not only hooks the reader, it entertains, builds momentum, and helps the story stay focused. But most of all, it casts a spell of anticipation that draws the reader on toward the story climax—toward the most important part of the story: THE MAIN EVENT.

CHAPTER 6

Discovering a Story's Main Event

· · · · · · · · · · · · · · · · · ·

or, What's it All About, Anyway?

L et's say a story begins with a bang, immediately drawing the reader in, capturing attention, and piquing interest. Next, the author allows the reader to fully experience the story world right along with the main character by skillfully weaving in plenty of well-written, specific, elaborate detail. Then a build up of suspense hooks the reader and moves the story forward. You'd think that with all of that story magic, the author couldn't miss, right?

Wrong.

Yes, a great beginning, terrific description, and some edge-of-your seat, nail-nibbling suspense are all-powerful tools for the author, designed to whet the reader's appetite for what is to come. But alone, these tools are not enough. All of the literary magic—the tempting, teasing, and tantalizing that has taken place—really serves to strengthen the implicit story promise: that the story is building up to something worth waiting for, or, as I call it, the main event!

The main event is what the story is *really* all about. It's the central problem, conflict, dilemma, struggle, or adventure that *changes the main character in some way*. It is a situation that forces the main character to grow, to learn something, or, at the very least, to have a change of heart. It's an event that carries significance—an occurrence that's *not* run-of-the-mill, that inspires some meaningful consequence. In short, the main event is what the story is really all about—*and it must be something worth writing about!*

Departure, Fulfillment, Return

In an interview with Bill Moyers, the late Joseph Campbell had this to say about the main event:

> "In popular novel writing, the main character is the hero or heroine; that is to say, someone who has found, or achieved, or done something beyond the normal range of achievement and experience."

Campbell goes on to describe the basic motif of the "hero journey" as "one in which the hero must leave one condition and find the source of life which will bring him forth in a richer or more mature condition." He speaks of this cycle as a transformation of consciousness brought about by trials or illuminating revelations. In short, according to Campbell, the main event involves departure, fulfillment and return.

This is not to say that every story must contain some fantastic, earth-shattering event. A person can grow and change—become a small hero—by extending herself in an extraordinary way within the realm of the ordinary.

Go Ahead, Make a Scene!

A main event is often referred to as a "scene." In a short story, there is usually a single problem or conflict, and so there is a single climactic scene followed by a resolution. Novels are usually constructed with a series of scenes, each building in intensity. The word "scene" probably conjures up images of the stage and screen. This is a helpful parallel for the writer. The scene, or main event, should be brought to life in a vivid way, told in a moment-by-moment, play-by-play, frame-by-frame style that could be acted out on a stage. The main event should unfold in a *balance* of action, description, and dialogue (external dialogue, which is talking, or internal dialogue, which is thinking).

How Authors Handle Main Event

Conflict, action, description, dialogue—these are the ingredients in the magical potion that makes main event. Look through the books in your classroom library and notice how the authors blend conflict, action, description, and dialogue to create memorable main events.

As an example, here is a scene from *Poppy*, by Avi, in which the evil owl, Mr. Ocax, kills and devours a rascally mouse named Ragweed.

Just then, Mr. Ocax pulled his wings close to his body and plunged. In an instant he was right above and behind the two mice. Once there, he threw out his wings—to brake his speed; pulled back his head—to protect his eyes; and thrust his claws forward and wide like grappling hooks—to pounce.

It was Poppy who saw him. "Ragweed!" she shrieked in terror as she hurled herself back undercover. "It's Ocax."

But the owl was already upon them. Down came his right claw. It scratched the tip of Poppy's nose. Down came his left claw. It was more successful, clamping around Ragweed's head and neck like a vise of needles, killing him instantly. The next moment the owl soared back into the air. A lifeless Ragweed—earring glittering in the moonlight—hung from a claw. As for the hazelnut, it fell to the earth like a cold stone.

Powerful but leisurely strokes brought Mr. Ocax back to his watching tree. Once there, he shifted the dead Ragweed from talon to beak in one gulp. The mouse disappeared down his throat, earring and all.

The author could have simply summarized the scene in a sentence—*Mr. Ocax swooped down, killed Ragweed, and swallowed him whole*—but that would have been nowhere near as compelling as the scene Avi wrote. (This is when the summarizing skills in chapter one become critical. Students *must* be able to recognize the difference between a summary and a fully elaborated main event!)

An interesting exercise is to project a story excerpt such as this on an overhead projector. Analyze the main event together with the class by reading it aloud and underlining action in red marker, description in green, and dialogue (including thoughts!) in blue. Students need to be able to differentiate between action, description, and dialogue before they attempt to write their own fully elaborated main event!

A Challenge for Student Writers

For student writers—perhaps all writers—the main event is the most difficult part of the narrative.

Like the rest of us, children are faced with numerous problems. However, it is usually the adults in their lives—parents, teachers, and other caregivers—on whom children depend to solve their problems for them. But in the world of literature, it's the main character, the protagonist, who must solve the problem. (This is, again, why the word *hero* is so often used to describe the main character in a story.) You can see why it can be difficult for children to draw from their own experiences in planning a main event in which the main character solves his own problem.

Another reason that writing a fully elaborated main event can be challenging for students (assuming they've come up with something significant) is because it involves combining all the skills learned to date. They must be able to define, differentiate between, and execute **action** (what the main character is doing), **description** (what the main character experiences through the five senses), and **dialogue** (what the main character thinks and says). I always teach main event *after* we've covered these other elements.

Children typically handle these challenges in one of several ways. I usually list, title, and define these less-than-successful approaches:

❖ **The Superman/Act of God Event.** In this situation, the author has come up with a serious problem for the main character but has no idea how to resolve it. So he or she resorts to a "Superman" resolution, or what the Greeks referred to as *deus ex machina* (literally *god from the machine*)—some Knight-in-Shining-Armor type comes along and solves the problem for the main character: *Finally Mom appeared on the Pirate Ship and took me home.* Sometimes, an act of God makes things right: *Just then the enemy space ship blew up and we were safe.* Readers accept this kind of situation (or suspend disbelief) only when the main character has truly struggled and earned that kind of a lucky break.

❖ **The Grocery List.** Instead of writing a single, significant main event, the author writes a grocery list of many insignificant and sometimes unrelated events. For example, the story might be about taking a magic carpet ride. Instead of relating what it's like up there in the sky and the significance it has for the main character—really bringing this adventure to life—she writes a list of "and thens": *First I flew over the whole town. Then I flew off over New York City and then I went across the ocean to France. Then it was time to go home.* Some-times this kind of grocery list is punctuated with an occasional editorial comment, usually of a general nature, such as *It was really cool* or *It was fun.* This kind of story can ramble on endlessly with little sense of satisfaction for the author or the reader. A good way to gauge the logic of a series of story events is to imagine shuffling them up. If the reordered sequence does not affect the story in any meaningful way, you've got a grocery list.

❖ **What? Another Problem?!** Students often think that they need to have a story problem and then make that problem worse. It's difficult for student writers to determine when a problem is bad enough and how and at what point the problem should get worse. The result is that they will often give their main character a problem—*I broke my mother's best lamp*—and instead of compounding or further complicating that situation (for most chil-dren, wouldn't breaking the lamp be enough of a problem?!) they introduce a whole new problem, often unrelated to the one before: *After that the cat got sick and I had to bring it to the vet.* This kind of thinking often sends the story reeling in another direction, which shifts the focus, confuses the reader, and weakens the plot.

❖ **What is the Point?** Some stories lack any kind of a main event at all. If the story can't be summarized in simple terms (*This story is about the time I lost my pet turtle during Mom's dinner party,* or *This is a story about my mountain climbing adventure*), then chances are the author either does not have something significant enough to write about or has a random series of disjointed events that lack a single focus.

Of course it's not enough to point out what *doesn't* work—students need to be provided with doable alternatives and a variety of strategies that will work for them.

Teaching Main Event

I gather the class in the library corner and open up another favorite book that I've been reading aloud to them, George Selden's Newbery Honor book, *The Cricket in Times Square.* I have timed my reading so that today I can share a main event with them. They settle down, and I read the following passage, which describes the escapades of a cat, a mouse, and a cricket who inadvertently start a fire at a newsstand in the Times Square subway station:

He couldn't see where he was going and he toppled over into a box of kitchen matches. A shower of matches fell around the shelf and onto the cement floor. There were several yellow bursts and the sharp scratch that a match makes when it's lit. Most of them fell far enough away from the wooden walls so they could burn themselves out without danger. But one match, unluckily, struck right next to a pile of that morning's newspapers. The spurt of flames it sent up lit the frayed edge of the papers and quickly spread over the whole bundle.

The children's eyes grow round. Some gasp and cover their mouths with their hands. "Oh, no!" they say. "Uh oh!" someone whispers. A few giggle nervously. I go on:

"Watch out!" shouted Chester. Harry Cat leaped up to the shelf just in time to keep his tail from being burned. The cricket was the first to realize what had happened—and what was likely to happen if they didn't put the fire out. "Get the Coca Cola" he said. "Pour it over."

"I drank it all," shouted Tucker.

"You would!" said Chester. "Is there any ice?"

Harry and Tucker dumped what was left in the insulated bag down on the flames. But it wasn't enough. The fire sputtered, died down and then flared up again, larger than ever.

"Maybe we can smother it," said Harry.

There was a pile of magazines on the very edge of the shelf, just above the fire. Harry strained and pushed and succeeded in toppling them over. They all peered over the edge to see if the fire was out.

"Oh fine!" said Tucker. "She's still burning and you blocked the hole to get out!"

They were trapped. Harry and Tucker jumped down and started pulling away the magazines furiously. But the fire crept closer and they had to back away.

"What a way to go," said Tucker. "I should have stayed on Tenth Avenue."

I glance at the children as I read. They are no longer in the classroom, cozy in the library corner. They have been transported to the subway station. I can see from their expressions that they can *see* the flames, *smell* the smoke, *feel* the panic of their small story friends. I continue:

For a moment Chester got panicky. But he forced his thoughts back into order and took stock of the situation. And an idea struck him. In one leap he jumped onto the alarm clock, landing right on the button that set off the alarm. The old clock began ringing so wildly it shook itself around the shelf in a mad dance. Chester hopped back to his friends.

"Any alarm in a fire," he said.

They waited, crouched against the wall. On the opposite side of the stand the flames were lapping against the wood. Already the paint on it had begun to blister.

Chester could hear voices outside the newsstand. Even at this hour there were always a few people in the station. Somebody said, "What's that?"

"I smell smoke," said another.

I watch the children begin to relax. They have lived this event right along with the main characters. They have felt the tension, moment by moment. And now they sense a resolution.

Chester recognized the voice. It was Paul, the conductor on the shuttle. There was a sound of footsteps running away, then running back again, and a hammering began. The newsstand shook all over.

"Somebody get the other side," said Paul.

The cover was wrenched off. Clouds of smoke billowed up. The people standing around were astonished to see, through the fumes and glare of the fire, a cat, a mouse, and a cricket, running, jumping to safety.

"Phew," someone says.

"That was a close call," says another.

They stretch and exhale in relief.

"You all really enjoyed that," I venture.

There is a hubbub of mumbled agreement. Many hands go up to relate fire stories of their own—the excitement, the fear, the aftermath. The feelings that this main event conjured up are very real, and they continue to linger.

As always, I pose my favorite question to them: "You know, boys and girls," I begin, "The author *could* have simply said, 'They accidentally started a fire and finally it was put out.' Would you have enjoyed that as much?"

The equivalent of a round of boo-hisses goes up. "That would have been boring," says John.

"Yes," I reply, playing the devil's advocate, "but that's what actually happened isn't it? They accidentally started a fire, and Paul put it out. How could that be boring?"

They continue to shake their heads and call out.

"There's no excitement that way," says one. "The way the author wrote it has talking."

"You call it dialogue and exclamations," offers another.

"And there was description too," says Alexia.

Casey is waving her hand wildly.

"Casey?" I ask.

"It's a *summary*," she says. "What you said about the fire starting and Paul putting it out is only a summary of what happened. It's not all the details."

I smile. They get it, even though they don't have a name for it yet.

"Yes!" I reply. "You are all right! The author cannot just give you a summary of something this important. The author has to help the reader to see, hear, smell, and feel the fire right along with the main characters. The author does this by mixing action, dialogue, and description. We call this a fully elaborated main event."

I go to the easel and write the following "recipe":

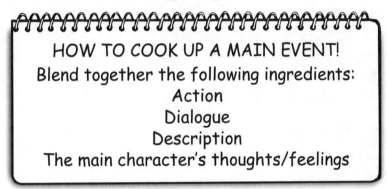

HOW TO COOK UP A MAIN EVENT!
Blend together the following ingredients:
Action
Dialogue
Description
The main character's thoughts/feelings

Then we roll up our sleeves and start "cooking." First I **MODEL** the procedure for them. I start off with a "summary" statement. It's always best to choose a topic that is timely and relates to some aspect of your curriculum. This ensures that your students will have sufficient background to contribute in a meaningful way.

"Too many Babas"

One of my favorite topics relates to a cute story the children read by Carolyn Kroll, "Too Many Babas." The story is about three Russian grandmothers who set about making a soup. But, as everyone knows, too many cooks spoil the soup! The grandmothers add too much of everything and have to start all over again, the second time with a careful recipe and plan. We talk about the main event in that story—how the main characters learned a lesson from their soup experience! We also brainstorm around my favorite main event question: "What could possibly go wrong?" We discuss all the things that might go wrong during a soup-making session. The children come up with lots of funny ideas. We finally agree that spilling the whole pot of soup could make a funny, entertaining main event.

I write SUMMARY STATEMENT on a piece of chart paper:

I spilled the whole pot of soup and made a big mess.

"All right," I say. "Let's think about how you might spill a pot of soup."

The children come up with a multitude of ideas—missing the counter with the pot, falling over a dog or cat with the pot in their hands, slipping on an area rug, tripping on slippers or shoelaces. (This is obviously something they've had some personal experience with!)

I choose one example that appeals to me: slipping on the area rug. Now comes the questioning.

"Okay, picture this," I say. "I'm walking across the kitchen with the big pot of soup. Is it heavy?"

"Yes!" they call out. "You're gripping on to it with big pot holders," says Sarah.

Cameron sits up very straight. "You're making a face like this because it's heavy." He demonstrates, grimacing and holding his breath. He also makes a grunting sound to emphasize my struggle with the heavy pot.

"Great thinking," I say as I begin writing.

I grasped the huge pot....

I pause. "What kind of pot was it?" I ask.

"Big and black," says Peter.

"Cast iron," says Emma, "Like the one my Grandma has."

"Terrific," I say as I continue writing:

I grasped the huge black cast iron pot with my old ragged potholders. "UGH!" I groaned. "This pot weighs a ton!"

"See the way I use quotation marks to highlight my words?" I ask. "See the exclamation?" They nod, knowingly.

"Okay," I say, "we've got action (*I grasped the pot*), description (*black cast iron pot);* (*old ragged potholders*), and dialogue (*Ugh! This pot weighs a ton!*)." I point back to the recipe chart. "Action, description, and dialogue! So far so good," I say. "But a main event also needs to be told in 'slow-motion,' with frame-by-frame action. We need to stretch out the actual falling part. Let's think about this. Can I have someone come up here and do a slow-motion pantomime of what it might be like to trip on the rug and fall?"

All of their hands fly up in the air. I call on an outgoing, uninhibited student. Jessica comes up, grinning ear to ear.

"First," she says, "you're walkin' along sort of heavy-like, because, you know, the pot is hard to carry." She demonstrates with Frankenstein-like plodding. She punctuates this with a series of grunts, groans, and grimaces. The class laughs, cheering her on.

"Then," she continues, "one foot hits the rug. It's an old, raggy rug, so your little toe gets tangled in the stringy stuff on the edge of it, and it pulls your foot." She drags one foot behind as though it were snared. At the same time she says, "But see, since you're caught in the rug you sort of tip a little this way..." She does an exaggerated rock to the left. "And then that way..." She tips to the right. "Then the soup, it starts to go gloop, gloop, gloop, all greasy thick soup slopping down the sides of the pot!" She opens her eyes wide and wobbles back and forth, pretending to steady the soup pot. "HOT! HOT!" she yells.

The class erupts in applause and laughter.

"Terrific job!" I say as I motion her back to her seat.

"Let me write down everything you did—that would be...?"

"Action!" they shout.

"Everything you described—we call that...?"

"Description!" they yell.

"And also, everything your character said—we call that...?"

"Dialogue! An exclamation!" they answer.

I continue writing. The result looks something like this:

> I grasped the huge black cast iron pot with my old ragged potholders. "UGH!" I groaned. "This pot weighs a ton!" I plodded on with heavy steps, every muscle straining with the weight of the pot. "Uhhhh!" I said, sweat forming along my brow, feeling very warm from the steam floating up from the hot soup. Suddenly (Suddenly *is what we call a red-flag word—a word that clues in the reader that something important is about to happen!)* my toe got snagged on something. I looked down. My poor little toe was stuck in the fringe that was unraveling along the edge of the old rag rug in the middle of the floor. I tipped to the left. "Woooh!" I yelled as the soup sloshed toward the edges of the pot. GLOOP! GLOOP! GLOOP! *(It's always fun to include a sound effect!)* The soup spilled over the edge of the pot as I tipped to the right. *(Notice the use of the word 'as' for the purpose of linking together two actions. It can also be used to connect dialogue and action, as in the earlier* "'Woooh!' I yelled as the soup sloshed...") Thick, greasy soup slopped down the sides of the pot. "HOT! HOT!" I yelled as the soup dripped over my fingers.

The children giggle, loving the play-by-play mix of action, description, and dialogue. I go on with the questioning. The questions might include:

❖ How does the pot actually fall?

❖ What kind of sound does it make?

❖ What would you say as it fell? *(Be careful—you might get some colorful answers!)*

❖ How does the kitchen look when the pot falls?

❖ Do you fall as well?

❖ What is your reaction to the spill? *(What do feelings look like?)*

❖ How will you clean it up?

❖ What did you learn from this experience?

Based on the answers to those questions, the finished, fully elaborated main event might read like this:

I grasped the huge black cast iron pot with my old ragged potholders. "UGH!" I groaned. "This pot weighs a ton!" I plodded on with heavy steps, every muscle straining with the weight of the pot. "Uhhhh!" I said, sweat forming along my brow, feeling very warm from the steam floating up from the hot soup. Suddenly my toe got snagged on something. I looked down. My poor little toe was stuck in the fringe that was unraveling along the edge of the old rag rug in the middle of the floor. I tipped to the left. "Woooh!" I yelled as the soup sloshed toward the edges of the pot. GLOOP! GLOOP! GLOOP! The soup spilled over the edge of the pot as I tipped to the right. Thick, greasy soup slopped down the sides of the pot. "HOT! HOT!" I yelled as the soup dripped over my fingers.

Then the worst thing of all happened. I felt the pot begin to slip, to slide in my hands. "Oh no!" I shouted as I gripped the pot handles tightly. But it was no use. The pot went flying out my hands. BOOM! It hit the floor. I watched, horrified as the soup splashed across the kitchen, an ocean of broth and vegetables covering the shiny white tiled floor. Tomatoes splattered against the cabinets. Carrots slid under the table. Potatoes rolled around like golf balls. My feet slid on the greasy mess and flew out from under me. My eyes popped open and my heart pounded. In a second, I found myself sliding through the whole mess on my backside.

"What a disaster!" I yelled. I sat there on the floor for a minute, my head in my hands. I'd better get rid of that rotten old rug, I thought to myself. After all, it was the cause of the whole problem. That's what gave me the idea. I grabbed the rug, sat myself down on it and pushed myself along the floor, mopping up the tomatoes, carrots, broth and potatoes. I scooped them up and threw them all away. Finally, I turned the rug over and wiped up the rest of the grease. Then I threw away the rug as well!

I looked around. The kitchen was almost as good as new. I made a decision then and there. The next time I wanted to have a nice hot bowl of soup, I'd go to a restaurant and order one!

After adding all of the children's suggestions, we read this together, analyzing for action, description, dialogue, and feelings. Of course, I ALWAYS refer back to the summary:

I spilled the whole pot of soup and made a big mess.

"Which is more entertaining," I ask, "the summary or the fully elaborated main event?"

The answer is unanimous—"The fully elaborated main event!"

Guided Practice

After modeling this procedure I give the children a chance to practice it. (You'll probably want to begin this on another day. If so, it's important to review the procedure and read through the example again.) Use the same summary statement about spilling the soup. Let students choose their particular problem for their main event—perhaps falling over a pet or tripping on the shoelace, whatever appeals to them.

Remind them about the kinds of questions they need to think about: what the character sees, hears and feels, what the mess looks like (told in at least three or four interesting sentences), their reaction to what happened, what they might think or say, and a solution. In short—what the main character senses, thinks, says, and does. Circulate as they work, asking these kinds of productive questions. Provide them with sentence starters if they need them. Read examples out loud. Play the cheerleader—really root them on!

We made a class book of the resulting main events, which we titled *Soup Trouble: A Collection of Main Events by 2M*. At right is eight-year-old Casey's example of her fully elaborated main event.

> Casey P. 2M.
> Baba Edis walked into the kitchen with the big pot of soup. It was so heavy! She scuffled with her shoes on the floor. Scuffle! Scuffle! She could not see with the big pot in her face. She tried to get it on the counter. "AA!" said Baba Edis. It was too late! She missed the counter! First her toe went in the air. Noodles were sliding on the floor. Tomatoes and potato hung from the ceiling. Carrots and celery slid down the walls. Baba Edis looked mad! She stood up with a big frown on her face! She crossed her arms. She put the pot away. Her dog ran in and slurped up the noodles on the floor. Her cat came in and ate the carrots and celery. Last, her rabbit came in and hopped up so high he could reach the ceiling. And the rabbit eat the tomtoes and potatoes. "Thank you" said Baba Edis to her pets. She also said "Good dog, good cat and good bunny!"

Application

In my experience, the main event is the part of the writing diamond that takes the longest for children to assimilate and independently apply to their writing. Usually, after children are exposed to these skills, they are quickly able to include an entertaining beginning, great elaborative detail, and even suspense in their process pieces. But for quite a while, they will continue to summarize or list the main event. This is only natural. The main event is a sophisticated blend of everything they've learned so far. They need to hear and analyze many, many examples from literature, and they need you to model the transformation of simple summary statements into a fully elaborated event. Give them plenty of opportunities for guided practice of this skill in isolation.

When I see a summarized main event in their process pieces, I simply underline it and tape another piece of paper alongside the page. I write down a series of relevant questions similar to those I used in the "soup" example. Then I have them go back and work through their event in "slow motion," praising their efforts every step of the way!

By the end of second grade, the majority of children can do this when it is presented in a very directed way, like the soup lesson. With continued modeling, practice, application, and encouragement most students can internalize this and apply it independently by the end of grade three.

Magical Transformations

You'll need a "whole bag of tricks" on hand for teaching main event throughout the school year. Here are a number of "Summary Statements" and teaching suggestions that you can use for teaching this skill.

SUMMARY STATEMENT

We went over the waterfall in the boat and survived!

TEACHING TIPS

The key to transforming this event is to stretch it out—tell it in a slow-motion mix of action (how you grip the edges of the boat, grab at nearby branches, shield your face, etc.), description (of the waterfall), the main character's reaction (what those feelings look like, what the character might exclaim), and the solution.

You take a ride on a magic carpet.	This is a main event that can become "listy." Have them choose a single destination rather than a list of destinations. Encourage the students to imagine what it is like up there in the sky (a description of the setting: Windy? Cool? Blue skies? Fluffy clouds?) and their reaction to flying (feelings, both physical and emotional, as well as thoughts or exclamations) and then introduce a problem. Ask, "What could possibly go wrong?" Write out that problem in play-by-play action.
You get chased by a space alien, but you get away.	Be sure to include a description of the space alien (how tall, what color, how many arms, legs, eyes; describe facial features, etc.) and your reaction to it. Then tell about the chase in frame-by-frame, slow-motion action. Include a sound effect or two and an exclamation from the main character. Be sure to tell how you feel during the chase.
You meet up with a dragon in a cave, and he breathes fire at you.	Describe the cave and the dragon (four or five sentences each). Include your reaction to the dragon and the cave. Does the dragon make any noise? Describe the flame and the temperature in the cave. Do you run from the dragon? Tell what happens in slow-motion, frame-by-frame action. What might you say during this experience?
The beautifully wrapped box that your grandma gives you turns out to have a puppy inside!	Describe the box (size, how it was wrapped, any sounds, movement, or other hints). Tell your thoughts—what you think or hope might be inside. Use the slow-motion, frame-by-frame technique to build suspense as you unwrap the gift. Include your exclamations. Finally, describe the puppy and your reaction. Be sure to tell what the puppy looks like (size, color, length and type of fur, etc.) and how the puppy behaves as you take him out of the box.

You can create summary statements like these around whatever theme you're working on, and then have your students magically transform them into fully elaborated main events! But the real magic occurs when students step back and see the results of their hard work—they truly come to see themselves as creative, capable writers!

CHAPTER 7

Writing Satisfying Story Endings

· · · · · · · · · · · · · · · · · · ·

or, All Good Things Must Come to an End

The author has tackled the main event, revealing a meaningful story problem or adventure through the use of action, dialogue, description, and feelings. It takes a lot of hard work to get to this place in the story, which is why the ending must not disappoint! The story ending is the icing on the cake, the neat knot that carefully ties up the story strands so that the reader can put the story aside with a sense of satisfaction. Hopefully, the main event will have brought about personal growth for the main character—perhaps by way of learning a lesson, forming an opinion, making a decision, or causing the character to wish or hope for something similar (or something very different) to happen again.

E.B. White certainly understood the need for a satisfying story ending. Read this touching conclusion to his classic book *Charlotte's Web*.

> Wilbur never forgot Charlotte. Although he loved her children and grandchildren dearly, none of the new spiders ever quite took her place in his heart. She was in a class by herself. It is not often that someone comes along who is a true friend and a good writer. Charlotte was both.

The ending consists of Wilbur's **memories** of the main event (Wilbur the pig's fantastic experience of being saved by Charlotte's web-writing), the main character's **feelings** (about Charlotte's children and grandchildren), and a **conclusion** or **decision** that Wilbur made (about Charlotte being in a class by herself and defining her as a good writer and a good friend). It is the kind of an ending that produces a deep, contented sigh, much as you might make after a wonderful meal, and a feeling of regret at leaving the story world behind. The feelings generated by a great story ending linger long after the story is through.

Beverly Cleary wraps up her ever-popular middle-grade novel *Ralph S. Mouse* with this passage:

> Ralph remained behind at the inn, where he rides around every night in his sports car, generously giving rides to his relatives and enjoying their company now that they have benefited from his education. He is strict about one thing, however. Ralph is the only mouse who sits in the driver's seat of the Laser XL7.

After reading Cleary's entire story, you can see how the ending sums up the development of Ralph's character. The word *generously* hints that perhaps Ralph was not always so willing to take his relatives for a spin. Taking that a step further suggests that Ralph has **grown** and **changed** in this regard. The fact that his relatives have "benefited from his education" also shows that, in the course of the tale, Ralph has **learned something**. "*He is strict about one thing, however. Ralph is the only mouse who sits in the driver's seat of the Laser XL7.*" These last two sentences are a good example of a **decision** that the main character has made.

Memories, feelings, personal growth—these are the ingredients that combine to make an effective story ending. Provide students with these ingredients to work with, and you give them alternatives to much less effective story endings such as:

❖ So that is the end of my story. THE END
❖ I went home and went to bed. THE END
❖ I woke up. It was just a dream. THE END

You also want to help them avoid some creative version of what I call the "superman" ending—another *deus ex machina* in which the story solution depends on some surprising, miraculous outside force that saves the day at the last minute.

Giving Students the Magical Ingredients for Story Endings

You'll want to plan this lesson for the day on which you read the children the ending of a middle-grade novel that they love. A favorite ending of mine is from Donna Jo Napoli's marvelous book *The Prince of the Pond*. I've got the children gathered around me as I read aloud. They are both eager to hear the ending and a little regretful at the notion of leaving these beloved characters. The combination of strong feelings leaves them rapt, their mouths slightly open, eyes wide, leaning forward as if to taste and savor every last word.

In this last passage, Pin (the frog prince) has been changed back into a man and his frog family (or 'fawg' family, as Pin used to say, struggling to control his newfound amphibian tongue!) must face and deal with their loss. I read slowly, carefully, almost reverently:

Somehow in that very moment I knew that Pin was gone forever. Jimmy was right—Pin had disappeared. I felt the strangest sensation of my life: A tear rolled down my cheek.

"Croak," said Jimmy in a tiny voice.

I looked at him. "Jimmy, you just croaked. For the very first time. Do it again."

Jimmy croaked a little louder. His left vocal sac inflated and deflated.

"I can croak, too," said another froglet. He croaked. His left vocal sac inflated and deflated.

"Me too," shouted another.

And the air was filled with croaks, as left vocal sacs inflated and deflated all around me.

"We'll be okay," said Jimmy. "We can protect ourselves. We can work together. We can help each other."

"Frogs don't help each other," I said automatically.

"But fawgs do," said Jimmy.

I looked at the hopeful little faces of my froglets. "Yes," I said. "Fawgs do."

The children sit motionless for a second, letting the feelings wash over them. Finally, someone utters, "Ohhh..." This gently breaks the spell, and the children begin to come back to me. The feeling of nostalgia for the story world they've just left is almost palpable. They stretch and murmur to one another. I overhear snippets of their comments; questions that they instinctively understand do not really require answers.

"Oh, that was SO good," says one student.

"Why couldn't he stay a frog?" asks another.

Several others pipe in. "You mean a FAWG. No, even though it was hard for him he had to turn back into a person."

"Maybe he'll visit the pond every day," says one of the girls, rather wistfully. Several students nod in agreement.

"So," I ask them, "how did you like the ending?"

"I didn't want it to end," says Jeff.

"Me neither," echo five or six others.

"Why do you suppose the ending was so satisfying?" I ask.

They think for a moment, uncertain.

"It just felt like it was supposed to end like that," says Amelia.

I turn to the chart paper, which is always hanging nearby. I title the page for them and begin jotting down some key points.

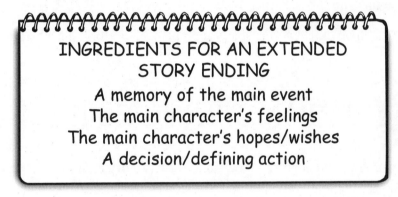

I introduce these techniques that authors use to write satisfying story endings. We briefly discuss each one, and I explain that the author can use any combination of these techniques to bring a sense of finality to a story.

Then I put a transparency of the following example on the overhead projector. We read the excerpt aloud together, sentence by sentence. As we read, I ask students which ingredients the author used, and I color-code each sentence by underlining with colored markers:

A memory of the main event—red
The main character's feelings—green
The main character's hopes/wishes—black
A decision/defining action—blue

> Doris the cat purred happily and curled up in the sunny window. She shivered a little when she thought about how long she'd lived in the streets as a skinny, stray cat. But that was then. Now she knew she would never again choose to wander about chasing mice like she used to. It would be fancy cat food for her from now on, served in a fancy glass bowl. As old Mrs. Winn patted her soft coat, Doris stretched and hoped that life would always be this good!

Our analysis would look something like this:

❖ Doris the cat purred happily and curled up in the sunny window.—**A Feeling**

❖ She shivered a little when she thought about how long she'd lived in the streets as a skinny, stray cat.—**A Memory**

❖ But that was then. Now she knew she would never again choose to wander about chasing mice like she used to. It would be fancy cat food for her from now on, served in a fancy glass bowl.—**A Decision**

❖ As old Mrs. Winn patted her soft coat, Doris stretched and hoped that life would always be this good!—**A Hope/Wish**

The children catch on quickly. This analysis prepares them for the next step in the process.

Revising BORING Story Endings

Now that we've seen and analyzed how authors write story endings, it is time to try our hand at it. As always, I begin by providing the students with a less-than-wonderful example, and I **model** a revision for them, asking questions to generate creative responses.

On a fresh piece of chart paper, I write the following story ending:

So, that is the end of the story about my big baseball victory.

"Okay," I say, "let's revise this boring ending. What do you think this story was about?"
"Winning a baseball game!" says John.
"Right," I answer. "Now let's use the ingredients for a satisfying story ending. Pretend you are the main character who has just won the big baseball game. Can you give me a *memory* of the most important part?"
"I'll never forget the crack of the bat as I hit that homerun," offers Dana.
I write that on the chart.
"Okay, how about telling me how you'd *feel* about hitting that homerun," I say. "A *feeling* is what we're looking for."

"Excited," yells Jackson.

"Terrific," I say. "Now somebody tell me what *excited* looks like!"

"I know," says Emily, "My heart pounded as the ball flew out of the park!"

"Great," I say as I write that down. "So far we have a memory and a feeling. What might you *wish* or *hope* for after winning a game?"

Jimmy begins, "I hope that..."

David finishes for him. "I sure hope we'll be just as lucky at our next game, too!"

I write furiously. "And how about a decision or an action that shows a decision?"

After a minute Deirdre pipes in: "You can be sure I'll be practicing extra hard for the play-offs next week."

Here's what our Before-and-After revision looks like:

BEFORE: *So, that is the end of the story about my big baseball victory.*

AFTER: *I'll never forget the crack of the bat as I hit that homerun and the way my heart pounded as the ball flew out of the park. I sure hope we'll be just as lucky at our next game, too! You can be sure I'll be practicing extra hard for the play-offs next week!*

Alternate Story Endings

As you read you will find that there are exceptions to this formula for creating extended story endings. Typically, in adult fiction, the main character's feelings and decisions at the closing of a story are *implied* rather than stated outright. For example, rather than saying that the main character feels hopeful and makes a decision of some kind, the author will *show* this through some *defining action*. (John takes a nasty spill off of his horse and, after much internal conflict, overcomes his fear of riding. The defining action might be John saddling up and mounting his horse.) Some of your more able writers may use the "defining action" quite effectively for a story ending.

Once in a while an author can use a more unusual device for an effective ending. Novelist Flannery O'Connor has said, "You can do anything you can get away with, but nobody has ever gotten away with much." This is certainly true of story endings. A trick ending of some kind, a challenging question for the reader, a powerful image—any of these can work but probably not as often or as easily as the memory-feeling-hope-wish-decision ending discussed in this chapter.

Dana

Camping

"Lights out!" I said. I was camping with my friend. "Lights out!" I yelled agan, off went the lights. The secint later we went to sleep. After a while I hard somerthing. It went Crach! Crach! Crach! I steped out sighd. The woods srrouded me. The black night hung in the sky like a tall bilding. The ground was mackylike quick sand. And leaves were all over the place. The next thing I knew something

1

big and ugly was be hind me. It had cloths around it. and it had red glowing eyes. It was a mummy! I ran as fast as the wind. I triped over a rock! splat! I fell strait in the mud. The mummy jumped on me. I could feel the bumpy cloth on me. I could feel his hot breth on the back of my neck. I sliped away just in time. I was wadering where was my friend. Then I riped of the mummy

2

cloth. Out burst my friend. Yelling "April fool's!" I thout I will get him back! But I wadered how did he get the red eyes to glow?

Dana's camping story has an unusual, entertaining ending that works. My attitude is, *If it isn't broken, don't fix it!* She tried something different, and it worked!

Before-and-After Activities for Revising Story Endings

The earlier baseball example is just one practice opportunity for children as they begin to experiment with effective story endings. There are a number of other applications of this idea which you and your students will find fun and stimulating.

1. Copy down a BEFORE ending in the middle of a large piece of poster board and label it. (A list of BEFORE endings appears at the end of this chapter.) Have students write their revisions on strips of lined paper. Cut them out and make a "revision collage" by gluing their AFTER versions all around the BEFORE renditions. Hang it in the classroom for their reference. (This also works as a bulletin board.)

2. Have students summarize a familiar story such as the Three Little Pigs, Little Red Riding Hood, or Snow White. Then have them write an extended story ending from the main character's point of view (without actually naming that character). Display these endings on a bulletin board and have class members identify the story based on the ending. For example: *She sat down, exhausted, after her escape through the woods. She would never forget the taste of that sweet porridge or the comfortable feel of the soft, fluffy beds. Even so, meeting that family of bears had been terrifying. She decided then and there that her days of exploring in the woods were over and that from then on she would not take anything without asking first!* (Goldilocks and the Three Bears)

3. Have students find story endings from books in your classroom or school library and identify techniques that the author used. Then have them rewrite the story ending using an alternate technique.

4. Have students take a completed story from their writing folder (either a process piece or a timed prompt) and look at their ending. Tape a "tail" to the edge of the paper and have them revise their own endings using a memory, feeling, hope, wish, or decision.

Remind students that, since they are only revising the ending and have not read the rest of the story, it is perfectly fine to make up some story details. If they are to include a memory, they might need to invent one—some sweet detail about Sugar, the dog, some particular characteristics of the animals at the zoo, or something notable about characters at the circus.

❖ So, after my big camping adventure I went home and went to bed. THE END

❖ Just as the space alien almost caught me I woke up. It was only a dream!

❖ So that is the story of my trip to the circus. THE END

❖ So, that is how I got my pet pony. THE END

❖ After all of that mountain climbing I fell asleep and slept for three days.

❖ That is why I like my dog, Sugar.

❖ We left the awesome zoo and went home. THE END

❖ That is the ending of my Halloween Witch story.

A Great Big Magical "AHHH..."

The feeling of satisfaction at magically wrapping up a story is not only reserved for the reader. Creating an effective story ending also brings about a sense of accomplishment, achievement, and success for the writer. The feeling of conclusion, the reflection on change and growth, the realization that the main character has become stronger, wiser, or more mature—all of these feelings and revelations (whether implied or stated outright) produce that great big magical "Ahhh..."—the "Ahhh" that transports us back to reality with a feeling that all is well again within the story world. That "Ahhh..." is the best measure of the effectiveness of a story ending.

Remember what Amelia said after hearing the ending of *The Prince of the Pond*? "It just felt like it was supposed to end like that." Author Patricia Reilly Giff captures Amelia's sentiments—and the great big magical "Ahhhh"—with this thought: "When I finally complete the book, it seems as if the story had always existed."

CHAPTER 8

Effective Dialogue

. . . .

or, To Talk or Not to Talk

Real, memorable characters talk. What they say reveals who they are and what they are like and gives us a glimpse at how they view the world. This is true in both real life as well as in fiction. It would seem, then, that writing effective dialogue would not be that hard. After all, we're surrounded by dialogue—conversation—all the time. However, story dialogue is very different from the kinds of conversations we engage in every day.

In her book *Dynamic Characters*, Nancy Kress observes: "Good dialogue, everyone agrees, seems natural. Note the verb: It *seems* natural. But in fact it's not." What Ms. Kress means is that story characters speak *selectively*, in a concise way, unlike in real life where we hesitate, repeat ourselves, and interrupt one another with disjointed snippets of ideas and information. An author chooses a character's words very carefully. When writing, the author must keep in mind the purpose of dialogue.

Dialogue should:
reveal something about the character *and/or*
move the plot forward.

Another characteristic of story dialogue is that it is usually interspersed with action, thought, and description.

A great example of effective dialogue comes from Katherine Paterson's Newbery Honor book *The Great Gilly Hopkins*. This scene involves the foster child, Gilly, and her social worker, Miss Ellis, on their way to Gilly's new foster home.

> Two traffic lights farther on Miss Ellis handed back a towelette. "Here," she said, "see what you can do about that guck on your face before we get there."
> Gilly swiped the little wet paper across her mouth and dropped it on the floor.
> "Gilly—" Miss Ellis sighed and shifted her fancy on-the-floor gears. Gilly—"
> "My name," Gilly said between her teeth, "is Galadriel."
> Miss Ellis appeared not to have heard. "Gilly, give Maime Trotter half a chance, OK? She's really a nice person."
> That cans it, thought Gilly.

You can see how Paterson skillfully mixed talk with action, thought, and description so that we get a sense of the tension between Miss Ellis and Gilly. We can also clearly see their respective personalities.

This is a very sophisticated skill, one that young writers really struggle with. Because children want to include dialogue in their stories, I break it down for them into three skill levels.

1. **Exclamation.** The author has a character exclaim something—usually a reaction to something significant in the story. Used in this way, an exclamation is really like thinking out loud. It does not require a response from another character. This is the first type of dialogue I have students use, and they usually experience great success with it. I insist that they "tag" their exclamations by using quotation marks, a word like "said", and the speaker's name. (*"Feet don't fail me now!" shouted John.*)

2. **Question-Action/Description-Response.** This next level of dialogue is more complex and requires two characters. The first character asks a question (or makes a statement). This is followed by a *related action or description* and then a response by the second character. All dialogue is "tagged." *("Was it you who broke that lamp?" asked Mom. <u>I shrugged and looked away.</u> "No," I whispered, hanging my head.)*

3. **Conversation.** Conversation is a longer exchange between two characters with action, thought and/or description in between. *("Was it you who broke that lamp?" asked Mom. There were shards of glass scattered all over the rug. I shrugged and looked away. "No," I whispered, hanging my head. Mom put her hands on her hips. "Well, if you didn't break it, then who did?" I glanced over at my dog, Red. He sat wagging his tail, the tail that had swiped the lamp off the table. If Mom knew that Red broke the lamp, she'd realize that I'd been playing with him in the living room. "Well," I said softly, "it was an accident.")*

I prefer that students are accustomed to using exclamations before moving to the next level— question-action/description-response. If they handle that well, have them expand the skill into conversation.

How to Help Students Generate Dialogue

I help students generate exclamations, questions/responses, or conversations by asking questions. If they are writing about exploring a haunted house, I might ask:

"If you were creeping through a haunted house, what might you exclaim?"
"It sure is spooky in here!" is one reply.

I'll write the exclamation on chart paper with quotation marks and a "tag."

"It sure is spooky in here!" I whispered as I crept through the haunted house.

We talk about the use of a specific verb (*whispered* as opposed to the more general verb *said*); the use of the magical connecting word *as*. I might encourage a student to insert an exclamation at several dramatic places in a story.

As students become proficient at writing exclamations, I move them toward **question— action/description—response**, again by asking questions. I often provide a framework like the one that follows.

question/response framework

"_____," _____asked.

_____
(An action or description)

_____," answered _____.

Here is a similar framework for **conversation**:

"_____," _____asked.

_____
(A thought, action, or description)

_____," answered _____.

"_____," _____ asked.

_____
(A thought, action, or description)

_____," answered _____.

This is a great way for students to think and write about what feelings look like, to think about body language and the ways in which our conversations are colored by facial expressions and gestures.

All Talk and No Action

Every year it seems that I have a couple of students who seem intent on writing their entire stories in dialogue. I call this "wire-tap" writing, as that is exactly how it sounds when read—like an overheard conversation. Here's an actual student sample of this kind of a story. You can see that the student started out by tagging all of the dialogue but soon lapsed into a "wire-tap." We cannot keep track of who is doing the talking. Action and description are implied through the conversation rather than being presented in contrast to it. Despite a very entertaining idea (an encounter with a skunk during a camping trip), the story gets buried in a jumble of talk.

> "Wow, this is a good night to go camping," I said.
> "Yea, but are you sure there's not going to be skunks in the forest?" said my older brother. He was a year older than me.
> Why should you be afraid?
> J...j...just trying to protect you, sis.
> Well get ready. We are going in a few minutes.
> Say bye to Mom and Dad.
> Let's go. Bye Mom and Dad.
> Wow, I didn't know there were so many trees in the forest.
> "Yea," said my brother.
> Now can we go home?

The story continues in this vein. Toward the end we find out that the writer, her brother <u>and</u> her sister were on the camping trip. In this particular piece, the student relies wholly on talk. I have had other students who tell their entire stories in *thought*—which is actually *internal* dialogue.

> *I think I'll go on down to the pond. It will be fun. I'll get my fishing rod and my net and walk over there. It sure is a nice day out. Maybe I'll catch a fish. I hope I do.*

In cases like these, students need to see and feel the difference between "wire-tap" talk and a balance of talk, action, and description. They also need to be offered an *alternative* to all talk and no action.

Translating Talk Into Action and Description

On page 127 of the Appendix is a lesson I present to students on All Talk, No Action. This lesson can help you assist students in identifying the problem as well as offering them practice in generating alternatives.

Dialogue adds so much to the magic of a story! A lively exclamation, which expresses feelings and reveals personality, can bring your characters to life.

WHEN WRITING DIALOGUE REMEMBER:

❖ Begin with simple exclamations at dramatic points in the story. Generate these by asking: "What might the character say in this situation?"

❖ When students are ready to handle more than one character, you may extend the exclamation to a question-action-response. Again, reserve this for dramatic parts of the story. Discuss gestures and body language. (Refer back to Chapter 4 on what feelings look like.)

❖ When your students have mastered question-action-response, extend this to a conversation interspersed with action, thought, and description.

❖ Beware of all talk, no action! Be ready to offer your students alternatives to this. You can help students convert "wire-tap talking" into action or description by modeling for them, using the examples in this chapter.

Getting in the Last Word on Dialogue

The magic show was almost over. "Abracadabra!" shouted the magician. (*An exclamation!*) He waved his magical pencil across the blank page. (*Action!*) A rush of wind blew a series of brilliant words across the paper. (*Description!*) His eyes grew round, and a smile crept across his face (*Description!*) as he carefully examined his work. (*Action!*) He turned toward his audience. (*Action!*) "It seems that I am an even greater maker of magic than I thought!" he said. A hush fell over the crowd. "How is that so?" asked a small girl in the front row. The magician looked proudly at the words on his paper and exclaimed, "It seems that besides being a magician, I have become a magical writer!" (*Conversation!*)

Enough said!

CHAPTER 9

Managing Your Writing Program

· · · · · · · · · · · · · · · ·

Managing a classroom writing program can feel overwhelming, especially when you consider the fact that writing is just *one* part of the school day. The teacher/magician must regularly juggle reading, math, penmanship, spelling, science, social studies, health and safety—an entire curriculum in addition to writing!

This balancing act was my biggest challenge when implementing my writing program. It just felt as though writing took forever. It would take *weeks* for me to conference with everyone—and that conference usually covered just one portion of each of their stories! I was constantly updating writing checklists that documented where students were in their stories, what their strengths and weaknesses were, and when they'd had their last conference with me. These checklists were never complete—as soon as I managed to meet with all my students, it would be time to begin the conferencing process over again to discuss their next story installment!

Whole-Class Writing Instructions

· ·

After regularly dropping a ball or two during my daily classroom juggling act, I decided to try delivering the basic writing lessons (those outlined in this book) to the *entire* class. I'd go maxi rather than mini and see what happened.

Whole-class writing instruction was appealing for many reasons. I could be certain that *all* my students received what I considered to be *assured* experiences in writing. The entire class heard me read through examples from literature (**define the skill**), watched and listened as I modeled the skill for them (**model**), and then attempted the skill themselves (**guided practice**). My entire class was exposed to a common writing vocabulary, which immediately enriched our classroom discussions and story critiques. Since lessons were very directed, there was little down time. Students were not as apt to get off track (as they tend to be while working independently and waiting for a conference).

SCHEDULING WRITING INSTRUCTION

I set aside two 40-minute blocks each week for whole-class writing instruction. During this time, I present skills in the *define—model—guided practice* format laid out in this book. This time was generally outside of my language arts block. I would use a portion of my language arts time for the *application of skills* in process writing.

In order to maximize classroom time, our process writing generally related to thematic units in our reading program. For example, when reading "Keep the Lights Burning Abbie" by Peter and Connie Roop (a story about a young girl who must care for and run a remote island lighthouse during a fierce storm while her father is stuck on the mainland), we spend some of our language arts blocks writing descriptions of a lighthouse in a storm. This provides students with a topic they have knowledge of, reinforces vocabulary taught in reading, and expands their vocabulary through writing. We might spend a half an hour of our language arts time twice a week for this kind of application.

In this way, we are not always working on an *entire* story but rather on an application of a given skill within a particular theme. Students really benefit from this—since the pieces they write are naturally shorter, we always have time for sharing. Children, especially younger students, are not as easily overwhelmed by the writing task when skills are presented in isolation. Students engage in conversations about what works and emulate the writing of others that they found particularly effective.

PROCESS WRITING

It is critical that children have the opportunity to process an entire story. They need time to think about the ways in which the skills they've learned can help express what they want to say as authors. They need to be able to play out the what-ifs in a story to see where their topics might lead them.

I generally present the class with a loosely based theme for their process writing. This theme is related to either a reading unit or a topic in science or social studies.

For example, we have a unit in our reading anthology called *Gifts and Treasures*. The stories in the unit are about all kinds of gifts and treasures—everything from giving and receiving material gifts to a piece on the Smithsonian Institute and the treasures it holds. We discuss what other kinds of gifts and treasures people can give and receive—gifts of time, of caring, of love, of freedom, and of nature. About halfway into this unit, I assign a process writing piece, something like, *Write a narrative story about giving or receiving a special gift.*

Students are free to integrate their favorite interest or hobby into this open-ended theme. A student who is fascinated with race cars might write about receiving a race car from an eccentric uncle. The child who has been begging for a dog will write about receiving a dog. Another might write a personal experience narrative about a special gift he's making for his grandmother. They can bring whatever they like to the task, and the variety is always amazing.

The common thread, however, is the narrative itself. They begin the writing task knowing the characteristics of a narrative. They understand that their purpose is to entertain an audience of others. They know that they might design a character/problem/solution story or an adventure story in which the main character must struggle, grow, and change. If they choose a personal experience narrative, they realize that it will require a good deal of description and feeling to take the place of the story tension of the character/problem/solution story.

Students begin with a story summary (using the frameworks for summarizing in the first chapter) that they will filter through the writing diamond. The diamond reminds them that they must include an entertaining beginning, plenty of elaborative detail, some sense of suspense leading to a single, significant main event, and finally an extended story ending. (Of course, earlier in the school year I don't expect to see all these elements—I only expect to see the skills that we've covered during our writing lessons to date.)

Knowing all this (and it is a LOT to think about as they begin writing!), I set them about their writing in a directed way. I break the process into incremental steps which take them through the writing diamond; this way, students will not become overwhelmed at the enormity of the task! I also try to provide a related art activity which students can move to as they finish each story section.

A Process Writing Timeline

Here is an example of what our process writing timeline might look like. Please note that each day of the process need not be consecutive. In fact, leaving time in between allows the students to tap into the subconscious in between actual writing.

Day 1	**Discuss theme** with students. Distribute summarizing frameworks and have students brainstorm topics and think about filling in their story summaries. Students may bring the summarizing frameworks home to complete. (About 30 minutes)
Day 2	Share our **story summaries**. Be sure each writer has a workable plan. (About 40 minutes)
Day 3	The entire class constructs individual, **entertaining story beginnings**. I begin by reviewing the menu for great beginnings, and I circulate as students write, sharing great examples aloud. (Remember, the actual beginning consists of only a sentence or two, and it should begin as close to the main event as possible!) (About 30 minutes)

Day 4	Students write their **description of setting**. (If their particular story takes place in a rather common setting, like a kitchen, skip this. Instead describe a story-critical **character** or **object**.) Before we begin, I review the questioning techniques for generating elaborative detail and remind them about sentence variety. I ask for at least three or four sentences of elaborative detail. I encourage them to include their thoughts and feelings as well. I circulate, offering individual help as needed and sharing various examples aloud. (About 45 minutes)
Day 5	Silently everyone reads over what they've written so far, checking for good word choice and story flow. Then I briefly review **suspense**—the Magic-of-Three, story questions, and word referents. I ask students to move on to a suspenseful portion of their story. I remind them that this does not need to be scary—it can be a sense of wonder or anticipation. (About 40 minutes)
Day 6	I review **main event**, reminding them to stick to one significant event and to stretch it out with a mix of action, dialogue, thought, and description. I have students begin writing their main events, and I circulate to assist them and read examples out loud. I do not expect that students will complete their main events during this session. (About 45 minutes)
Day 7	Students read over their stories silently. I have some students share aloud. Then I instruct them to complete their **main event**. They will need a **solution** to a story problem or a **conclusion** to a story adventure. (About 45 minutes)
Day 8	I review **extended story endings** and have students write through to the end of their stories. I encourage them to go back and make any revisions they might need. Typically this involves taping a paper strip "tail" to the edge of a given story page for the addition of an exclamation, thought, or description. I might underline a story-critical character, setting, or object that they've neglected to describe or a feeling that they've told rather than shown. (45 minutes)
Day 9-10	Read stories aloud—**peer critiquing** and suggestions. (40 minutes per session)
Day 11	**Final revisions**. Since I've been circulating during each writing session, I have met with all of my students daily throughout the process. Few lengthy individual conferences are needed. (40 minutes)

Throughout the 11 days, I have been circulating throughout the class, and have pointed out spelling and punctuation errors that children can correct on their own (words and skills we've learned) or written in the correct spelling and punctuation that we have not yet covered. This way, if we decide to go ahead and publish the pieces, the children's final drafts are already corrected and ready to be copied over.

Following this kind of a timeline eliminates the need for complicated checklists. Children also reap greater rewards because they are all working on a given section of their stories at the same time. Reading the sections that they have all been working on reinforces the particular skill, making sharing more relevant.

With this approach, your entire class could complete a process piece in several weeks. These could be published in a class book as a collection of short stories around a given theme.

Writing as a Link to the Unconscious

I'm just flabbergasted at what my unconscious mind knows that my conscious mind doesn't know. It's what you tap with fiction, and it's scary.
—*Sophie Burnham, novelist and fiction writer*

The first few times that I assigned my class a process piece on a given theme, I worried that perhaps even that much structure, however loose, might interfere with their ability to express themselves freely in meaningful ways. As an author, I understood that writing is a lot more than skills alone. It has everything to do with the heart and the soul. It has to do with expressing what is most important to you. And I sensed that it had something to do with tapping the subconscious. But it wasn't until I had completed my beginner reader, *Witch Way to the Country*, that I truly understood the meaning of Sophie Burnham's words.

There are two central characters in my story—Druscilla the Witch, who is tall, lanky, loud, spontaneous, careless, messy, adventurous, and modern, and her cousin Constance. Constance the Witch is short, plump, careful, methodical, neat, cautious, quiet, and old fashioned. I thought it would be great to add story tension through their opposite personalities. Anyway, that's how I *consciously* created them. But as I sat back and read the finished, published book I had a revelation. It became apparent to me that I wasn't really just writing about a couple of interesting, fun story characters pulled out of my imagination. What I saw for the first time were the characteristics of my husband's and my respective personalities! The struggles and tensions my characters faced in their story mirrored, at least in essence, struggles and tensions in our relationship, and in the end my two story characters put their differences aside and understood that their affection for one another overshadowed everything else. (And, no, I won't tell you which character I resemble most closely—I'll let you guess!)

I have since seen the same magical thing happen to student writers. After eight months of instruction in this program, I asked a group of third graders to write a narrative story about finding an unusual egg. They were to brainstorm where they might find an unusual egg, what might hatch from it, and what kind of a problem or adventure might result.

One little boy was quite immature for his age, developmentally much more a second grader than a third grader. His story was about finding an egg in his back yard. A cute, little bunny hatched from the egg. The boy teaches his new pet how to use a pencil and the bunny completes all of the child's schoolwork for him. It is a story with a happy ending.

This boy did not just write an amusing, cute fantasy story. Instead, he discovered that a story can express truth—hopes, wishes, and dreams—in a very satisfying way. He expressed, very poignantly, the frustration of his days in school and his desire for things to be different.

A girl whose parents were in the midst of a difficult divorce wrote about being in charge of a group of construction workers digging a trench. They unearth an unusual egg, which begins to hatch. A menacing creature emerges from the egg—a half man, half serpent—which she hits with a shovel, thus saving everyone she is responsible for.

This child *really* wrote about her needs to affect her situation and to express her anger and her desire to save those she cares about. It is a story that was unleashed from her subconscious and expressed through metaphor. Her skills as a writer allowed this to take shape.

In other students' stories, I also found that if you scratch the surface, you look deeply into the child's thoughts. Reading these stories put to rest any concern I had about thwarting children's ability to communicate by assigning a "theme." On the contrary, the skills, structure, and underlying diamond pattern served as a powerful framework through which students could go beyond the literal and tap the heart and soul through the subconscious.

Prompt Writing

Prompt writing is intended to be an objective tool for assessing student writing. Students are given a specific time frame (usually 45 minutes) within which they must write a story to a given prompt. Here is an example of a narrative prompt intended for fourth graders.

> **Imagine that you are exploring your grandmother's basement on a rainy day. You find an old trunk down there. Tell what is inside and what happens next.**

Their stories are later scored according to a **rubric**—a numerical score-point scale with each number defined by a set of objective criteria. For a sample of my rubric, see page 115.

The scoring is done holistically—the scorer treats the piece of writing as a whole, looking for the overall impression that the writing delivers. Spelling and mechanics are not scorable elements in these stories. The emphasis is on the story's meaning and how well it was expressed.

Students take about five minutes to look over the prompt and then spend the next 40 minutes writing. The idea is that whatever writing skills they have mastered will be evidenced in their impromptu writing. When administered periodically a teacher can gauge a student's growth and progress. Administering prompts too frequently (I have been told that some schools administer a prompt every week!) defeats the purpose, since students do not have enough time in between to practice and assimilate new skills and apply them.

Prompt Analysis

Part of a student's ability to respond successfully to a prompt involves being able to analyze what the prompt is asking for. I always ask students to distinguish between the **given** and the **variable** elements in a prompt. The given elements are details provided in the prompt. The variable elements are details that the writer needs to determine. Let's look again at the prompt about the trunk in grandmother's basement. I might use this to teach children how to distinguish between the given and variable elements of a prompt.

Imagine that you are exploring your grandmother's basement on a rainy day. You find an old trunk down there. Tell what is inside and what happens next.

GIVENS	VARIABLES
Main character: You—a first-person story	What you find in the trunk
Setting: Grandmother's basement	What happens next—your problem/ adventure (Main Event)
Plot: Discovering trunk and contents	**Ending:** Solution or Conclusion

Once the students decide on the variable elements, I ask them to formulate their ideas into a **summary framework**. Their story plan might look like this:

This is a story about my exploring my grandmother's basement on a rainy day. The adventure begins when I find a magic carpet in an old trunk and go on a magical ride. After a scary ride it brings me back safely to grandmother's basement.

Next, on the basis of the prompt I'll ask students to think about the **story-critical character, objects, or setting** that deserves to be described in detail. (Think of Barry Lane's magic camera—what would be worthy of a magic photograph?) I have students list at least two things that they will describe in detail. (In this prompt it would be logical to describe the basement, the trunk, and what you find inside.) I always provide students with the following:

General Rules for Prompt Writing

❖ Analyze the givens and variables.

❖ Make a story summary to work from.

❖ Name at least two story-critical elements to describe in detail.

❖ Spend no more than five minutes planning. Remember: it does not have to be your favorite story, just one that works.

❖ Channel your story summary through the writing diamond.

❖ Begin your story as close to the main event as possible. (If your story takes place in the basement, begin there. Do not begin with getting up in the morning!)

❖ Write about one single event, not a list of events.

❖ Read over your story and save five minutes at the end for revision.

Pacing During Timed Writing Experiences

The 45-minute time limit generally enforced during timed impromptu writing can be extremely intimidating to the student writer. In order for children to approach the task in a positive way, we need to provide them with some pacing skills.

I use prompts instructionally to give the students a sense of pacing, so the assessment tool itself does not interfere with the assessment. I will assign the class a prompt, explaining that we will work through it together within the given time frame. I also use this as an opportunity to review all key skills.

Imagine that something very unusual happens while you are visiting the zoo. Write about your zoo adventure.

I write the following time chart on the board:

PROMPT WRITING PACING

5 minutes: Plan
10 minutes: Entertaining Beginning/Description of Setting
20 minutes Suspense/Main Event/Solution/Conclusion
5 minutes: Extended Ending
5 minutes: Reread/Revise
45 minutes: TOTAL TIME FOR EXERCISE

Now, at first this means very little to the children—elapsed time is still such an abstract concept for them. To make it a little more concrete, I sometimes place colorful sticky dots directly on the clock face indicating the transition point between the steps above. This eliminates the need for children to have to constantly watch the clock and count around in five-minute intervals.

1. Explain that following this time sequence will help them finish their prompt on time. Use a race analogy. A runner must pace him/herself in order to finish. What happens if a runner falls behind in the first part of the race? (They need to pick up the pace during the latter parts of the race.) Explain that it is the same when writing to a prompt. If a particular part of the story takes longer, they may "borrow" from the next time slot. Of course, if you borrow from one time slot, it leaves you less time for the next story section!

2. Be sure to have the WRITING DIAMOND on display for their reference.

3. The ground rules include using every available minute. THEY MAY NOT ASSUME THAT THEY HAVE DONE THEIR BEST WORK UNLESS THEY HAVE USED THE ALLOTTED TIME TO COMPOSE, REREAD, AND REVISE.

4. Distribute the prompt. Explain that they will have exactly five minutes to plan their story. (You may provide them with a summarizing framework and ask them to list at least two story-critical settings, characters, or objects that they will describe in detail.) Watch the clock—have them begin together and give them a three-minute checkpoint. **Stop them at the end of five minutes.**

5. BRIEFLY review great beginnings. Remind them to begin as close to the main event as possible, and begin with either:

> ❖ A SOUND
>
> ❖ An ACTION (Put the character in the setting doing something.)

❖ THOUGHT or QUESTION

❖ DIALOGUE or EXCLAMATION

BRIEFLY review elaborative detail. Remind them to include at least three or four sentences with good sentence variety to describe the setting and draw the reader in. They should freeze a moment in time and use the five senses for observation purposes. Remind them that they will have exactly 10 minutes to accomplish this. (Really play the cheerleader—lots of positive, you-can-do-it encouragement!)
BEGIN TIMING (10 minutes). Give them a five-minute checkpoint.

6. **Stop them at the end of 10 minutes.** Remind those who may not have finished that they will need to pick up the pace (borrow) during the next sequence.

   BRIEFLY review SUSPENSE. (Don't give it away too soon, ask story questions, use word referents, or the Magic-of-Three.)

   BRIEFLY review MAIN EVENT. Remind them that they must stick to ONE SINGLE event—and elaborate on that by stretching it out. Write the following "recipe" on the board and remind them that they MUST include all of the following in their MAIN EVENT:

   ❖ SLOW-MOTION, PLAY-BY-PLAY ACTION

   ❖ DESCRIPTION OF OBJECT OR SETTING (three or four sentences)

   ❖ AN EXCLAMATION

   ❖ A SOUND EFFECT

   ❖ THE MAIN CHARACTER'S FEELINGS/REACTION

   BEGIN TIMING (20 minutes). Give them five-minute checkpoints. At the last five-minute checkpoint, remind them that they must conclude their adventure.

7. BRIEFLY review the elements of the EXTENDED ENDING. Write the following recipe on the board:

   ❖ A MEMORY OF THE MAIN EVENT

   ❖ A FEELING

   ❖ HOPE OR WISH

   ❖ DECISION

   Remind them that if they have not yet concluded their main event, they must use some of their final five minutes in order to do it. This will require them to move ahead more quickly or borrow from their final five minutes. **BEGIN TIMING (10 minutes). Give them a three-minute checkpoint.**

8. Congratulate them on their stamina and hard work! Explain that they have five minutes left. If they have not completed their extended ending, they'll need to do that first. Instruct them to read over their entire story, looking for each part of the writing diamond. Insert interesting words or phrases. Add punctuation. Check for untagged dialogue—add "he said" or "I said" as necessary.

Begin timing (5 minutes). Give them a three-minute checkpoint.

9. Ask who has finished. For any students who have not finished, find out which section set them behind. Address this with a prescriptive lesson. (You may want to circulate and monitor them as they work through each section to see who has finished in time. Taking a particularly long time to write a given section may be an indication that they need to review that skill.) Congratulate them and collect their prompts!

This entire pacing lesson takes about a solid hour (45 minutes of actual writing time, plus the mini-reviews before each section). You do not need to do this often—maybe once early on in the year and once again at the end of the year. In this way, children get a feel for the 45 minutes and can move their stories along accordingly.

Timeline and Scope and Sequence

I've included the following timeline and scope and sequence for writing instruction, which was used with great success at Mill Hill School in Southport, Connecticut. Using this schedule of instruction proved to be powerful in many ways. It guaranteed that all grade two and three students would benefit by common, assured experiences in writing. They acquired skills in a logical, sequential manner, one skill building upon another. By grade four and five, students have internalized the writing diamond, and they begin to take creative liberties with it. As our Connecticut Mastery Test scores clearly show—92% of our students reached the mastery level in 1997—this kind of consistency definitely pays off in student achievement.

While this scope and sequence was written for use in grades two and three, it can be used successfully in any two consecutive years of school.

TIMELINE/SCOPE AND SEQUENCE FOR WRITING INSTRUCTION
Grade 2

September:

❖ First week of school, introduce three kinds of writing through the use of selected picture books; from then on, identify everything you read accordingly. Summarize everything you read using the summarizing frameworks (Reading/Writing connection).

❖ Introduce the writing diamond. Use examples in literature as examples of each section of the diamond.

❖ Introduce, model, and practice elaborative detail. Have students write an entertaining description of something relevant to what you may be reading or studying.

October:

❖ Introduce great beginnings—read examples that work, model a revision using each technique, provide guided practice.

❖ Begin a middle-grade novel read-aloud, pointing out how the author uses each skill. (*Prince of the Pond* by Donna Jo Napoli and *Poppy* by Avi are highly recommended.)

❖ Review, model, practice writing elaborative detail.

❖ Administer a narrative prompt. Talk it through, decide what information the prompt provides, outline what decisions students need to make (givens and variables). Review the writing diamond. Remind them to write an entertaining beginning and to include at least two elaborative segments of a story-critical character, object, or setting.

November:

❖ Introduce techniques for building suspense. (Define, model, practice).

❖ Review great beginnings and elaborative detail.

❖ Begin a process piece. Pick a theme and talk through story plans. (Students use a summarizing framework to do this.) Have the entire group work on beginnings one day, description of setting the next, etc., sharing and dialoguing as they proceed.

❖ Casually discuss main events and endings as their stories take them there.

December:

❖ Introduce/model/practice main event.

January:

❖ Introduce/model/practice effective endings.

❖ Practice all previously taught skills in isolation (e.g., create a class book of suspense pieces or descriptive pieces).

❖ Continue reading great middle-grade material (*The BFG* or *George's Marvelous Medicine* by Roald Dahl).

February—March:

- ❖ Work on revision in all skill areas.
- ❖ Type up and discuss student prompts and process pieces with constructive suggestions for revision.

April:

- ❖ Work on a process piece. (This is a great time for writing an Egg Tale—a story about finding an unusual egg.) Look for all elements taught. Reteach as necessary. Share and discuss this work.

May—June:

- ❖ Review, reteach skills as needed. Administer a timed prompt to pass along to the grade three teacher.
- ❖ It is especially nice, after a whole year of instruction, to have students choose their favorite piece of writing and look it over again with their new-found skills. We often have a writer's tea or formal reading day with invited guests for the purpose of sharing this work.

Grade 3

September:

- ❖ Review the three kinds of writing, writing diamond, and all its parts.
- ❖ Administer a prompt as a diagnostic tool. Talk it through with students; let them plan it a day in advance. Tell them that you'll be looking for each section of the writing diamond. Guide them through it and help with pacing (e.g., "You probably should be moving toward your main event," or "You have 20 minutes left").

September—November:

- ❖ Review/model/practice entertaining beginnings, elaborative detail, suspense, main event, and effective endings.
- ❖ Administer a monthly timed prompt for diagnostic purposes. Double score with a colleague.
- ❖ Begin reading middle-grade novels aloud, highlighting skills used. (*Cricket in Times Square* by George Selden, *Turn the Cup Around* by Barbara Mariconda, and *James and the Giant Peach* by Roald Dahl are good choices.)

November:

- ❖ Begin a process piece. Pick a theme and talk through story plans. (Students use a summarizing framework to do this.) Have the entire group work on beginnings one day, description of setting next, etc., sharing and dialoguing as they proceed.

December—May:

❖ Revisit all skills previously taught—reteach, present opportunities for further practice and application in isolation (e.g., a book of elaborated main events or suspense vignettes), and complete process pieces.

❖ THE FOCUS IN GRADE 3 SHOULD BE WORKING ON THE CULMINATION OF SKILLS NEEDED TO WRITE A FULLY ELABORATED MAIN EVENT.

Throughout the Year:

❖ Revision exercises as needed, Before-and-After activities, prompts as needed. (We do one a month in Grade three.) Continue reading, discussing high-quality middle-grade novels and citing skills used.

At the End of the Year:

❖ It is especially nice, after a whole year of instruction, to have students choose their favorite piece of writing and look it over again with their new-found skills. We often have a writer's tea or formal reading day with invited guests for the purpose of sharing this work.

Narrative Writing Rubric

0- <u>Unscorable</u>! Wrote nothing or did not write to the prompt.

1- <u>Lots of room for improvement</u>! Way too short. No details. Doesn't make sense. Hard to read and understand.

2- <u>Still has a way to go</u>! Shopping list. Too short. Hard to understand. Not enough details and interesting words.

3- <u>Still needs work</u>! It has a *little* bit of detail but mostly general details like nice, good, red, blue, very, etc. It has an okay beginning, middle, and end. Lacks a single entertaining MAIN EVENT! Does not include the main character's feelings or reactions. Needs more elaboration to make it interesting.

4- <u>Good</u>! Has definite beginning, middle, end. Has some specific elaborative details. Stays focused on the important events. Includes evidence of most parts of the writing diamond.

5- <u>Great</u>!! Has a strong beginning, middle, and end. It is interesting and entertaining. Stays focused on the important events. Has sentence variety, many specific details, interesting words, descriptions of story-critical setting, character, and/or object. Includes the main character's feelings and reactions.

6- <u>Fantastic</u>!! <u>Wow</u>!! Has a great beginning, entertaining middle, and strong ending. There is strong evidence of every section of the writing diamond and lots of great description! Author uses interesting words and sentence variety. There is a mix of action, description, and dialogue. This story is smooth and easy to read. Reads like a "real" book.

—© Empowering Magical Writes 1998

The Most Wonderful Writing Lessons Ever
Scholastic Professional Books

Putting It All Together

The journey to becoming a writer is a long one but a journey well worth taking. When you begin this journey as the tour guide, the facilitator, as the *teacher*, the whole undertaking can seem exciting but also overwhelming.

However, here is the magic. No matter where you happen to be on your journey now, as you move through the lessons, the conversations, and the activities in this book, something amazing will begin to happen. You will begin a transformation. You and your students (whether you're one step or many miles ahead of them) will become a community of writers!

What feels awkward as you embark becomes, step by step, second nature. What feels difficult and complicated at the onset becomes demystified and doable, skill by skill. What feels new and cumbersome at the beginning becomes familiar, comfortable, even graceful with practice, patience, and persistence.

Newbery Honor author Patricia Reilly Giff always says that writing is not some mysterious, innate gift that only a privileged few possess. She insists that it is a craft that can be learned by anyone at all.

So, congratulations! You are already on the road to becoming a writer! Be sure to enjoy the magical journey!

Name: ....

Read the story beginning in the box below.

This is a story about the time I took a wild roller coaster ride.

It is BORING! It will not capture the reader's attention or make the reader want to read on. REVISE it using one or two of these ideas:

☀ **Action:** Put your character in the setting DOING something.

☀ **Dialogue/Exclamation:** Have your character SAY something.

☀ **Thought/Question:** Use your character's thoughts or questions.

☀ **A Sound:** Use a sound effect.

REMEMBER: Begin as close to the main event as possible (getting on the roller coaster) and DO NOT write an entire story! Just write the beginning sentence or two!

_____

_____

_____

_____

_____

_____

(Go on to the back if you need more room.)

Name: ....

Read the description in the box below.

The description of the pirate is *general*. The author didn't give us any *specific* details.

REVISE it by writing a six to seven sentence description of the pirate. Be sure you use good sentence variety to answer the following questions about the pirate:

- ☀ How big was the pirate?
- ☀ What did the pirate wear? (pants, shirt, jewelry, hat, shoes)
- ☀ What color and type of hair did the pirate have?
- ☀ What kind of facial expression did the pirate have? (eyes, nose, mouth)
- ☀ How did the pirate move?
- ☀ What did the pirate carry?

_____

_____

_____

_____

_____

_____

_____

(Go on to the back if you need more room.)

The Most Wonderful Writing Lessons Ever
Scholastic Professional Books

Name: ....

Read the description in the box below.

It was a nice fall day in the forest.

The description of the forest in fall is *general*. The author didn't give us any *specific* details.

REVISE it by writing a six-to-seven-sentence description of the forest in the fall. Be sure you use good sentence variety to answer the following questions about the forest:

- What grew there?
- What were the trees/leaves like?
- What kinds of animals did you see/hear?
- What was the weather like? (temperature, wind, rain, sun, clouds)
- What did you hear/feel/smell there?
- How did you feel about being there?

_____

_____

_____

_____

_____

_____

(Go on to the back if you need more room.)

The Most Wonderful Writing Lessons Ever
Scholastic Professional Books

Name: ....

Read the description in the box below.

> Jim looked really mad.

The description of Jim's anger is *general*. The author didn't give us any *specific* details.

REVISE it by writing a six-to-seven-sentence description of how Jim looked. Be sure you use good sentence variety to answer the following questions about how Jim felt:

- ☀ How did his mouth look?
- ☀ How did his eyes and eyebrows look?
- ☀ How was he standing?
- ☀ What did he do with his hands/feet?
- ☀ Did he make any sounds?
- ☀ What else about Jim told you he was mad?

_____

_____

_____

_____

_____

_____

_____

(Go on to the back if
you need more room.)

Name: ....

Read the discovery in the box below.

> When I went in the basement I saw a ghost.

The author gave away some exciting information too soon. REVISE it by using the Magic-of-Three to lead up to the discovery. Use this pattern—be sure to use three different hints.

1st Hint: You see/hear/feel something.
You try to discover what it is, but find nothing.

2nd Hint: You see/hear/feel something again.
You try to discover what it is, but find nothing.
Include your reaction!

3rd Hint: You see/hear/feel something still again.
You try to discover what it is and make your discovery!

There I was tiptoeing through the damp, dark basement.

_____

_____

_____

_____

_____

_____

It was a ghost!

Name: ....

Read the story ending in the box below. It is the ending of a story about being lost in the woods. It is abrupt and boring.

Once I found my way out
I went home and went
to bed.   THE END

Imagine what it was like being lost in the woods. Imagine how it would feel to find your way out. REVISE this story ending using at least three of the following ideas:

   ✿ A MEMORY of being lost

   ✿ A FEELING describing what it's like to find your way back.

   ✿ A HOPE or WISH about the future (because of what happened)

   ✿ A DECISION you'd make because of what happened.

   ✿ A DEFINING ACTION you'd take that shows what you decided.

_____

_____

_____

_____

_____

_____

(Go on to the back if
you need more room.)

Name: ....

This is a story about _____
main character's name

The problem was that _____
describe problem

_____

_____

_____

_____

_____

The problem was solved when _____
Tell how main character solves the problem.

_____

_____

_____

_____

_____

The Most Wonderful Writing Lessons Ever
Scholastic Professional Books

Name: ....

This is a story that describes _____
an experience or a place

_____

_____

First, _____
Describe what happens in the BEGINNING of the story.

_____

_____

_____

Next, _____
Describe what happens in the MIDDLE of the story.

_____

_____

_____

Finally, _____
Describe what happens in the END of the story.

_____

_____

_____

The Most Wonderful Writing Lessons Ever
Scholastic Professional Books

Name: ....

This piece gives information about _____

the topic

_____

Including _____

a main idea

_____

_____

_____

_____

another main idea

_____

_____

_____

_____

and _____

another main idea

_____

_____

_____

_____

The Most Wonderful Writing Lessons Ever
Scholastic Professional Books

Name: ....

Read the summary of the main event in the box below.

> A shark swam around
> me but I got away.

This should be a scary, exciting event, but it is boring to read. REVISE it by using the following "recipe":

- ✿ Slow motion, frame by frame ACTION
- ✿ A three or four sentence DESCRIPTION of the shark
- ✿ Your THOUGHTS and FEELINGS
- ✿ An EXCLAMATION
- ✿ A SOLUTION or CONCLUSION

_____

_____

_____

_____

_____

_____

_____

(Go on to the back if
you need more room.)

Name: ....

All Talk and No Action

Stories are not exactly like real life. Real life is often not entertaining—but narrative stories should be. In order to make your narratives entertaining you must choose every word carefully. You must have a **BALANCE** of description, action, and dialogue

You must avoid using as much dialogue as you might hear in real life—remember, stories are not meant to imitate real life, but to highlight the entertaining parts.

Here is a conversation from a story. It is hard to follow and the reader loses interest quickly.

> Hi! Hi! "What are you doing today?" I asked. "Not much," said Dave. "Want to go fishing?" "Okay, let's get our stuff." "I'll get my rod and my tackle box." "Don't forget the bait." "What do you have for bait?" "Night crawlers, what else? Want to see them?" "Yuck! They are so ugly!"

Now read this revised version. It has a **balance** of description, action, and dialogue.

> I saw Dave walking toward me. It was a warm, sunny day and I was happy to meet up with a friend. Dave was always ready for an adventure.
> "Hey, Dave!" I called. "Want to go fishing?"
> Dave waved and strolled over to meet me. He nodded and smiled. "Great day for fishing," he said.
> We both went to get our gear, first to my house. I dragged out my old bamboo rod and the worn green metal tackle box. At Dave's we headed for the basement. He opened the old refrigerator and held out a coffee can. "Check these out," he said.
> I peered into the dented can and wrinkled my nose. The can was filled with brown wavy seaweed-like stuff that looked alive! The whole mass was squirming around the bottom of the can like something out of a horror movie.
> "Night crawlers," said Dave with a grin. I jumped back.
> "Yuck!" I answered. "They are SO ugly!"

127

All Talk and No Action (page 2)

Here are some examples of how to transform dialogue into action or description.

DIALOGUE	ACTION OR DESCRIPTION
"Hi!" I said. "Hello," she answered.	We said hello.
"That's one ugly dog!"	The dog was the ugliest I'd ever seen, with huge drooping ears, bloodshot eyes and a pushed-in piggy snout.
"I hope I don't fall off this cliff!"	I stared over the edge of the cliff and gasped. It was at least a hundred-foot drop onto the jagged rocks below. I backed up, careful to keep my balance.
"Get your things packed!" "Okay."	My mom reminded me to start packing. I jammed my clothes into the old brown suitcase and slammed it shut.

Now it's your turn. Read this pasage of dialogue. Revise it. Decide on what will be most entertaining as dialogue. Then tell the rest with action and description. Write your revision on the back of this page.

"Please, Mom, don't make me babysit!" "You have to!" "But little Earl is such a monster!" I said. "That isn't nice!" "I'm going now, so you watch little Earl!" "Little Earl, don't do that!" "Oh no, now you've done it!" "You've spilled the grape juice all over the white couch! Now I have to clean it up before Mom comes back!"

(You could describe little Earl, use action to show Mom leaving and Little Earl spilling his juice. Describe the mess on the couch. Decide which line of dialogue is the most entertaining. That's the line to leave in!)

The Most Wonderful Writing Lessons Ever
Scholastic Professional Books